Marion L.

Halt!
I'm a Federal
Game Warden

HALT!

I'm a Federal Game Warden

The Amazing Career of
"The Toughest Game Warden
of Them All"

**Willie J. Parker
with Conway Robinson**

Foreword by Nathaniel P. Reed

DAVID McKAY COMPANY, INC. New York

Library of Congress Cataloging in Publication Data

Parker, Willie J
Halt! : I'm a Federal game warden.

1. Parker, Willie J. 2. Game wardens—
Tennessee—Biography. I. Robinson, Conway,
joint author. II. Title.
SK354.P37A35   363.2 [B]   77-10493
ISBN 0-679-50779-5

10 9 8 7 6 5 4 3 2 1
Manufactured in the United States of America

Foreword

WHEN I ASSUMED the office of Assistant Secretary of the Interior for Fish and Wildlife and Parks in May 1971, I had never heard of Willie Parker.

No sooner had I arrived on the scene than Willie Parker's name became very familiar. He turned out to be a highly controversial federal game management agent.

Willie had worked himself up the ladder, as a member of the Tennessee Game and Fish Department, as an undercover agent, as a federal warden, and finally as "agent in charge" for the state of Maryland and Virginia's Eastern Shore. He was assigned to the Eastern Shore District in January 1966. His duty assignment included the prime waterfowl areas for the Washington-Baltimore area. It seemed that everyone in government, the Congress, business, or the lobby shot waterfowl on the Eastern Shore, and all too frequently they either broke or bent the federal Migratory Bird Treaty Act regulations.

Willie was sent with firm instructions to clean up the area. Baiting, over-limit hunting, night hunting, and market gunning were common occurrences. Good agents had come and given up. The federal judges were known to have a deaf ear and a closed eye to federal indictments for illegal waterfowling.

Willie, recognizing the adage "punishment must fit the crime," persuaded the federal prosecutors and judges that continued illegal waterfowling would destroy a great natural resource and that they must share the responsibility for the protection and maintenance of the great flights of waterfowl that have made the region justly famous.

The more I heard of Willie, the more I was convinced that he was just the man necessary to stop the crescendo of illegal waterfowling.

Interior Secretary Rogers C. B. Morton came from the Eastern Shore and gave me strong support, which made it possible to dodge the flack of outraged hunters caught shooting over bait or with bags far in excess of legal limits.

Monday mornings during the waterfowl season, my phone rang off the hook with errant hunters and their lawyers requesting appointments. Men swore their innocence in my office, then pled guilty when Willie presented the evidence in court.

Willie Parker is a tough, noncompromising man who wears the badge of courage. His life has been constantly in danger, yet he has never been intimidated. He is motivated by a genuine concern for waterfowl and the future of the resource.

If there are to be ducks, geese, and swans in numbers comparable to what we know today, there must be Willie Parkers, men who enforce the law without regard to who you are. The combination of habitat protection, law enforcement, and a strong hunting code ethic can guarantee the continuance of the sights, sounds, and smells that make waterfowling such a special sport.

Nathaniel P. Reed
Former Assistant Secretary for
Fish and Wildlife and Parks
U.S. Department of the Interior

Author's Preface

THEIRS IS A profession that has, for the past one hundred years, been responsible for the protection of our wildlife resources.

These people, known across the nation as conservation officers, game wardens, special agents, fit into many molds, yet have one concern in common.

Some wear blue uniforms, some wear tan uniforms, some wear green uniforms, and some wear no uniforms at all.

But, beneath their badges, in their hearts they all have an undying desire to protect the wildlife resources of this nation, resources that are becoming more important to us all every day.

These conservation officers form a thin line that stretches across the North American continent and they stand guard between the wildlife of America and those people who would seek to exploit these resources.

The nation is indeed greatly indebted to their service.

This book is dedicated to one simple premise: to give credit to the conservation officers of the United States, credit that they seldom receive.

I hope through its reading, this story will afford an idea of what these wildlife protectors do, how they do it, and why.

Willie Parker
Special Agent in Charge
U.S. Fish and Wildlife Service
Nashville, Tennessee

Contents

Halt! I'm a Federal Game Warden

chapter 1

The Old Man
of the Marsh

I WAS LOOKING across the saltwater marsh on Maryland's Eastern
Shore with my binoculars when I saw this old man coming across an
open stretch of brown sea grass. I could easily determine that he was
a very old man because I could see him clearly and I watched him
for a good long time.

He was running a line of muskrat traps, zigzagging through the
grass, skipping the potholes, moving directly to each trap.

But I could see that he carried his shotgun with him. "Evidently
hunting goose," I thought. It was cold that day. It was very cold.
There was a skiff of snow on the ground and hunting activity had
almost stopped, so I waited until the old man came out. When he
hit the road, I stepped up and introduced myself to him. "I'm Willie
Parker, federal wildlife agent."

He carried a couple of black ducks and he had five or six
muskrats. In checking him, I determined that his old shotgun was
completely unplugged, allowing him more than the three legal
shots.

He was astounded when I told him that he was breaking the law.
He shook his head as if he just didn't understand. "I've been
hunting with that gun ever since I bought it in the early nineteen
hundreds." It was one of the old model pump guns. I could see that
all right. If he bought it in 1900, it was at least sixty-five years old
and it looked as if it had been used hard for every one of those years.

This man was a typical Maryland Eastern Shore marsh man. He
had on waders (hip boots) with the tops folded down. He wore
canvas hunting trousers, an old flannel shirt, and a mackinaw. He
didn't seem to notice the ice particles that were frozen to his rough
beard.

I explained the regulations to him, relating to the need for having a plug in that gun. "I've been hunting with that gun for some sixty years or more and I ain't never tried to put more'n three shells into 'er."

I asked him for his license. This was in 1970, the first year that the state of Maryland had put out complimentary licenses for aged people. I read that license. This man was eighty-eight years old! He had on an old hunting cap with the fur muff extended down over his ears so that it was difficult to tell just how old he was by looking at him. I did notice that he still had all his teeth!

I looked at that old man and then looked at that old gun and thought, "Well! Eighty-eight years old!" He was just standing there alongside that damn marsh road with a sort of bewildered look on his face like he really didn't understand what was going on.

"How many times, Chief, have you been arrested during those eighty-eight years?" I asked him.

"I ain't never been arrested."

"Well," I replied, "I don't feel like starting you down that road now. I think that I'm going to take this information from you and request that the United States attorney decline to prosecute you, but I guess we'd better plug that old gun."

"Well, that's fine," he nodded. So we got some tools out of my car and we plugged his gun so that it would only hold three shells, according to law.

But something held me there. I motioned to an old log that lay alongside the marsh road. "I wonder if you would mind talking for a while, Chief?" I could see that his mind was very alert for an eighty-eight-year-old, even though his face and hands were weathered by countless harsh winter days like this that he had spent on the marsh.

So we sat down on that log and he was most congenial, very talkative. He told me stories that I will never forget. He was born and reared on Kent Island, Maryland, just a short distance up bay from where I had run into him.

All of his life he had been a waterman. He had done nothing during his entire life but oystered, crabbed, fished, trapped, and hunted. He went from one thing to the other according to the season.

He told me that in his boyhood days they didn't need a calendar; they could determine the time of the year and what seasons were about to come on them by the appearance of the wild ducks. He was talking about the migratory flights of the canvasback duck during the time around the early 1900s when the canvasback was one of the prime, most valued waterfowl on the Chesapeake Bay.

That was the duck that both the market hunters and the sportsmen sought. The old marsh man explained that they used to wait days and days and days. Maybe once in twenty years, the canvasback would arrive from the north country to their wintering grounds on the Chesapeake Bay a week early.

But they always kept a careful watch because these were the ducks for the family to eat as well as those killed for the market. The old man said that at the first of November, the ducks would begin to come. But they always waited for the canvasback. These would come in dribbles at first; you'd see them. And then, he said, by the fourth or fifth of November in a normal year, the canvasback would literally blacken the skies. He said that they would pass for days and days on end. Solid canvasback ducks overhead. Flying fast and flying high.

I'm reasonably sure from my experience as federal wildlife agent on the Atlantic Coast that many of these birds were going as far south as Florida, many of them were dropping off in North and South Carolina, but countless thousands of them were staying to winter in the land of the Chesapeake Bay—on the Eastern Shore of Maryland.

The old man sat there on that damned log and he told me about hunting. He told me about hunting trips that were unbelievable. He told me about killing 120 canvasback ducks a day. "We used to put out about five hundred pounds of corn twice a week. 'Course it was legal in those days to bait the ducks." He said that he always had one cove where he and his father or his brothers could kill 125 canvasback with little or no trouble at all in a day's hunting.

Now the amazing thing about this man. Even back in those days, prior to the time when federal regulations governed the taking of canvasback and other wild ducks, the people of the marsh would only kill as many birds as they would need and no more, and *they* didn't shoot but three days a week. They would sell what they shot on the market for about twenty-five cents a duck and they would still have plenty to eat.

Even at that time when the wild ducks, especially the canvasback, were plentiful, this old man of the marsh had an active interest, a compassion for wildlife. This was a part of his life. He told me that he remembered when the Migratory Bird Treaty Act was first put into effect. I think he told me that the first thing they did was to put a twenty-five-bird limit on the ducks and he said he could recall his father telling him, "Son, it's over, it's all over." This was somewhere in 1916 or 1917.

But the ducks still came down each autumn in tremendous numbers. The old man said that they had good shooting for another forty years.

He told me about living a whole year when the total cash outlay for his entire family—and there were five children besides himself and his mother and father—would be less than fifty dollars. "We lived on the ducks," he said. "We lived on the land."

It amazed me as we sat on that log on that cold January afternoon. He had an old pipe and he'd fire that pipe up and his hand, when he was lighting that pipe, was just as steady as a rock.

Finally he got up and left and I sat there on that log alone thinking about the things that he had told me, about the sky being blackened with great flocks of wild ducks.

After he had gone, something made me look up at that gray evening sky. Maybe it was the whistling of ten thousand wings. Maybe, but when I looked, I saw nothing except a flight of about five geese fast disappearing to the east and I knew then that I had made no mistake. My life had already been dedicated to the protection of our wildlife, our natural resources. There was just no other way to go.

I was born and reared on a tenant farm in Fisher Hollow, near

Greenbrier in Robertson County, Tennessee, and most of what we had to eat in those days of my childhood, when I was a small boy in a large family of a tenant farmer, we got by hunting and fishing.

chapter 2

"Pa, I Seen a Rabbit Settin' "

MY FIRST ASSOCIATION with hunting started, I guess, with my first memories of anything. I can remember my father coming home from a hunt with birds, squirrels, rabbits, all sorts of game—game that made up an important part of our meals in those early days. We were a very poor farm family.

I distinctly recall the first gun that I ever fired. It was a single-barrel Winchester shotgun that kicked me completely to the ground when I touched it off.

This excited me because I knew that one day I would be large enough to take that gun and go off in pursuit of game. This happened before I was seven years old.

We got our drinking water from a spring that was some five hundred yards from the house and my duty every morning just at dawn was to take two large, four-gallon buckets to the spring, dip them full of freshwater, and haul that water back to the house for cooking and drinking purposes.

On my way over to the spring one early November morning, I saw a rabbit. I remember there was one hell of a frost on the ground. I froze in my tracks when I saw this rabbit.

He was at the edge of a little garden patch that sat on the north side of Long Branch. We lived in an old farmhouse about a hundred yards from Long Branch.

The rabbit hopped across this bottom and went under a brush pile at the edge of the field. I waited for some five minutes and he didn't come out.

I went on to the spring and got the water and hurried back to the house. I must have spilled about half of it before I got there, I was so excited, and I ran into the old farmhouse.

"Dad! I know where there's a rabbit!"

"Well, son, I'll get the gun and go kill it."

"No! Let me kill it!"

"Bill, you think you're big enough to handle that Winchester?"

"Yes, sir!"

He gave me one shell. I never will forget that shell. It was red. I got that gun out and my hands trembled. Down across that back field I went, across the foot log, across Long Branch.

After I got across the foot log, I was still some fifty yards from where I had last seen this rabbit. I cocked the old gun. It took both hands to cock it, pull the hammer back. I couldn't get the stock up to my shoulder. The stock was just too long. So it had to fit under my right arm.

I was praying that the rabbit was somewhere else as I sneaked up to that brush pile. It wasn't that I minded killing the rabbit. It was simply that I wasn't sure I wanted to tangle with that big shotgun that morning.

I walked up to that brush pile with the gun barrel stuck up in the air and me holding on to it with both of my small hands and I kicked that damned brush pile.

Well, that brush pile exploded. That rabbit came out of it like a flying ball of fur and across the edge of that bottom he went and up the hillside.

I pointed that twelve-gauge shotgun in his general direction and touched 'er off!

And when I got up off the ground, I looked and there was that rabbit rolling off of that hillside.

I had killed it!

I ran to where the animal lay at the bottom of that hill and I touched its soft fur. I picked it up very carefully and walked slowly to the house with my prize. I was so proud of what I had done.

My mother took me in her arms and said, "That's my mighty hunter!"

She and I went out behind the house and she showed me how to skin and clean it and then take it to the stream and wash it off.

That evening for dinner, we had quite a feast. My dad had killed a couple of rabbits the day before, but the rabbit that I killed was cooked separately from those other two rabbits and I got the choice piece, the back strip. I never will forget that meal! We had fried rabbit and hash-browned potatoes and piping hot biscuits and we all drank black coffee because that's all we had to drink.

If there never had been any other indoctrination into the wonders of nature, that one experience would have been all that I needed to start me out in a career that was to put me in close daily contact with the out-of-doors and the wildlife that I loved.

It's a strange thing, but a prophecy written in my high-school yearbook stated that I would someday be a wildlife conservation officer in Robertson County, Tennessee, and damned if this didn't come true!

chapter 3

A Badge and a Gun

AFTER HIGH SCHOOL, the Second World War took up all of my time and attention. As a naval bombardier, I spent considerable time in the South Pacific. I won the Air Medal and the Distinguished Flying Cross. I got out of the navy in 1946, farmed for a year after that, but I saw there was no future looking seven days a week at the ass end of a mule, so I went to college for two years under the G.I. Bill.

By now, I was married to my high-school sweetheart, Faye Gibbs, and we were living on only ninety dollars a month and had a young daughter at that.

One evening, State Senator Lige Darke came to the house and asked, "Bill, how would you like to be a game warden? This is really not much of a job, but we've never had a man from Greenbrier to hold a state job and it's important to the Democratic party that we do; it would be good politics. If you are interested, I want you to go to Nashville and talk to E. C. Tayloe, the director of the Tennessee Division of Game and Fish."

I was interested in the job and did go to see Mr. Tayloe the next morning.

"Mr. Parker," he said, "the salary for game wardens is one hundred and forty dollars a month. You have to be at least five feet eight inches tall and you have to weigh at least one hundred and fifty pounds."

Well, I was a half an inch under the minimum and only weighed 125 pounds, but Mr. Tayloe gave me the job anyway.

"You go on back to Greenbrier, Bill, and we'll get in touch with you."

"Fine."

About a week later I received by mail a badge and a commission signed by Tayloe. I also got a lawbook and a pad of arrest report forms, and hell, I was a Tennessee conservation officer. This was in the spring of 1949 and I didn't worry about my weight, thinking that they'd forget all about the physical examination.

There was no training for the job. No training whatsoever for those first months. I bought a secondhand thirty-two-caliber pistol, it was an automatic, and I bought me an old 1933 Ford and I went to work.

But if being a game warden suited me, it didn't suit a lot of other people in Greenbrier.

There was this old man from my hometown named Williams, Tom Williams. Tom was an institution in the village. He wore bib overalls and an old felt hat and he chewed tobacco. He ran the only concrete block machine in the county at the time and I worked for him once in a while. He always wanted me to stay in college.

One day he came up to me on the street and when he got rid of his whole cud of tobacco against the curb, I knew he meant business.

"Bill, I heard you took a game warden's job!"

"Yes," I said. "That's right, I have."

"Bill, that's no job for you! You don't want a damned job like that, why that's terrible!"

"Well, Mr. Williams," I answered, "I think I might want to do this. I think it might serve a very useful purpose."

He took another chew off his plug. "Look, son, you don't want that job. Hell, you'll have to *hire* pallbearers. You won't have enough friends to bury you if anything happens to you."

And I replied, "Well, I'll just have to take a chance on that."

Williams shook his head sadly. "I still want to turn you against this idea, Bill, 'cause it's very bad. My God, boy! We don't want a game warden in this town. No, we can't afford to have one here. None of the fellows are going to want this, especially the ones that hunt and fish!"

"Well, they're just going to have to get used to it, I guess."

Old Tom Williams stuck his hat way back on his head and let go a stream of Brown's Mule tobacco. He wiped his mouth on his coat sleeve and looked hard at me. "Well, I'll tell you one thing, son, and this is my final shot. If it don't make you turn down that damn job, then I just don't know what will. Boy, before I'd take a job as a game warden, I'd just as soon pick shit with the chickens to make a living. I just wouldn't do that!"

Well, I went ahead with the job anyway and I found in those early days that this deep-seated resentment was shared by about eighty percent of the people in Robertson County, Tennessee. They cut the tires off my car; they cut the radiator hoses off my car; they would call my house at every hour. They harassed me and they harassed my family.

But this wasn't all of my problems. About the twentieth of November of that year (1949) I got a surprise letter in the mail. I was instructed to report to Nashville headquarters for an official weighing and measuring session on December 2. Hell, I thought that they had forgotten all about the fact that I was twenty-five pounds underweight. I was feeling fine. In perfect health.

Well, I began frantically to try to gain weight. It was miserable. My weight was already just about suited to my height, but I had to put on more just to satisfy some Tennessee bureaucrat I guess, but in any event I was about eight and a half pounds underweight the day before the weigh-in. It was scheduled for nine o'clock in the morning and this is very early in the day to try to adjust your weight. I'd been told about, and finally decided on, a crash program of eating bananas because they were weighty and would compact if they were chewed up. Bananas and chocolate milk shakes! This was my only chance!

About thirty minutes before I went up for that weigh-in, I ate better than five pounds of bananas and drank either three or four large chocolate milk shakes. And when I got up there before the doctor who was conducting this weigh-in, I was deathly sick. I was just about to heave. I weighed 149½ pounds, had missed my mark by a damn half a pound!

I looked at those scales and he looked at me. "You are a half-pound underweight!" I could barely talk because I was so full, but I managed to ask him if he would consider giving me an extension of time to try to gain that half a pound. He was very considerate and he said, "I'll just go ahead and list your weight as one hundred and fifty pounds." It was all I could do to hang around long enough to thank him.

"I have to go!" And I had to, just as soon as he certified me. I *had* to go because I was deathly ill. As soon as I found the nearest rest room, I unloaded five pounds of bananas and four chocolate milk shakes and it was two years before my normal weight reached 150 pounds!

The first man I encountered in my official capacity as a conservation officer for the state of Tennessee will be etched in my memory for as long as I live.

There was a closed season on game fish in the state of Tennessee at that time, and I ran across this man sitting there on Red River, bank fishing. He was sitting on a board that was lying across the top of a seven-gallon lard can.

"I'm Willie Parker, state wildlife officer. Have you caught anything?"

"Nope, haven't caught a thing," he answered, but just then I heard some fish sloshing around inside that lard can and so I asked him to get his ass off the can, which he did.

There were four smallmouth bass in that can. His mistake was filling that damn can about halfway up with water.

"This is a violation of the law for you to take those fish at this time of year. I'm going to have to write you up."

Well, my God, he started crying!

"Look!" he told me, "I've really got a problem. I've got a wife and six kids. I haven't worked in nine weeks and am really not able to work. I had an automobile accident and I've been very sick."

He was still crying.

"We're destitute to the point you wouldn't believe. In fact, I came out here to try to catch enough fish for those kids to eat."

Well, by now, he was actually crying; tears were running and this really affected me. I thought, "Hell's fire, if I'm going to have to deal with this kind of a situation, with this kind of people under these circumstances in the profession of game warden, well then, it's going to be very bad."

I listened to this man tell his whole story and it got worse as he went along. The rent was way overdue. Doctor bills were piling up, hospital bills had him buried, and his family was crying, "No clothes!"

I finlly said, "Well, my God! Let's turn the fish loose and I won't charge you."

But he shook his head, "Well, that's supper for my little kids."

And I thought, "Well, Great Gods, I really have been put in a decision-making spot on my first case!" I was apprehensive in this situation, my first official dealings with a member of the hunting and fishing fraternity.

"Well, I really don't know what to do. This is my first day on the job, but I think I'm going to let you take the fish." He left just about the same time that I did.

While I continued working around the county, I agonized over the decision that I had made. These were illegal bass taken in closed season and I let this man get away with breaking the law.

Several hours later, the old car that I was driving developed a growl in the transmission. I stopped in a country road service station outside Greenbrier and pulled right in on the rack.

As I got out of that car, I heard the damndest laughter I had ever heard in my life. There were ten or twelve people standing around in the front part of that service station and they were all howling! I stopped in the doorway to listen and find out what was so damned funny.

I looked through that door and there was the same man I had encountered on the riverbank and whom I had let take home the four smallmouth bass, and this is what I heard him saying:

"Boys! You wouldn't believe it! I told that dumb son of a bitch that I had a wife and six kids, that I hadn't worked in nine weeks, and that we were all on the point of starvation!"

Everybody in that damned station was just howling, rolling on the floor. The man kept on. "And I even cried some for him and I thought that damn dumb warden was going to cry, too. He told me,

'Let's turn those fish loose and I'll turn you loose too,' but I said, 'No, I've got to have them fish to feed my little kids and . . .' "

Well, I stood in that doorway just astounded at what I was hearing. Then I heard this man say, "If that dumb son of a bitch knew that I had five hundred dollars in my wallet while he was talking to me and that I'm foreman down at the woolen mills, he really woulda been madder'n hell, wouldn't he?"

I don't even recall what happened in the next few minutes, but I forgot all about the trouble with the car.

I went inside that service station and I got ahold of this man and I threw him in the damned car and I hauled his ass forthwith to the county courthouse at Springfield.

He was the first man I had ever arrested. I told Judge Swann the whole story, what had occurred at the river and again what I had heard at the filling station.

The judge fined him fifty dollars and costs and I left that courthouse with a great feeling of satisfaction.

I also left there with my first lesson in law enforcement. From then on I would deal exclusively with the facts of a case and never let emotions interfere with my official business.

chapter 4

The Red River and
Terrapin Ridge

OLD MAN TOM STEWART lived on a rundown hillside farm up on Red
River right next to the Kentucky state line. It was one of those
marginal farms with its fields about as skinny as Tom's old mule
was and its weather-beaten, ramshackle buildings just as
swaybacked!

And Tom was a typical southern mountaineer, too! Bib overalls,
blue denim shirt, felt hat that was stained with sweat, a week's
growth of whiskers—the whole thing. By the looks of his place, he
spent more time fishing than farming.

Spring was his favorite time for being on the river because
noodlin' catfish was his sport. A catfish noodler wades the cold
waters and reaches up under a riverbank where the fish are laying,
spawning. He reaches carefully up under a fish and grabs it by the
gills. Noodlin' catfish is a cold, muddy sport, but it's effective.

Some of those good people up on the Red River caught catfish by
this method that weighed as much as fifty or sixty pounds.

About this time, I think it was during the spring of 1950, when I
had been on the job a little less than a year, Tennessee made some
regulatory changes concerning some of our conservation laws and
one of the most important made the noodlin' or tickling of catfish
illegal.

Well, I took it on myself to drive that old Chevy of mine around
those backcountry roads, stopping in at all the farms to explain the
new law pertaining to the noodling of catfish. I told those country
folk that they just couldn't do this anymore.

This news came as a great shock to a lot of these people. For over
a hundred years back, ever since this country was settled, they went
to the river each June to noodle catfish. It was a big deal for these
people, but the state of Tennessee decided that this practice wasn't

good for the catfish because it was taking the spawning fish right off the nest.

So I went on up on Red River one day and stopped in Tom Stewart's place to tell him the sad news. He was sitting there on the sill of his kitchen doorway whittling on a stick. I got out of the car and walked over.

"Tom, they've passed a law that prohibits the taking of catfish with your hands."

He didn't say anything for a while, just kept right on whittling on that damned stick. Finally he threw it down, snapped his pocket knife shut, and put it in his pocket. He shook his head.

"Well, Bill, that just about does it! It looks to me that the damn state of Tennessee has selected just about everything that I like to do and has made it against the law! First they stopped us from gigging. Then they stopped us from using a seine, and now, by God, they've stopped us from noodlin'!" The old farmer shook his head sadly. "There's very little left!"

Well, I sort of felt sorry for the old man, so I showed him how to use a fly rod. I finally made a fly fisherman out of him and after a while he became a real good friend and supporter. We had many a long talk about the old days when they used to take fish in unlimited quantities by various methods that are all illegal now. It took a lot of talking to convince Tom and his friends that conservation practices and their compliance with the game laws made sense in the long run and would help them as much as anybody.

There was a strong feeling against controls on hunting and fishing as set by the state. "Them damned fellers ain't got no business on my land," was the general attitude and it took four or five years riding those back Tennessee roads like a gospel preacher to get the point across—that I was going to enforce every fish and game law on the books.

This section of Tennessee, Robertson County, where I first worked as a conservation officer, was fantastically beautiful country. It was green rolling country with miles and miles of clear running streams, Class A smallmouth bass waters, and thousands of farm ponds that were filled with largemouth black bass. And the streams were full of catfish, redhorse, white suckers, redeye, bass. There was just about everything a fisherman could ask for here and all kinds of small game and just about everyone in these middle Tennessee counties hunted and fished, but they had to be educated.

Those early days on the job were both fun and nerve-racking. There's a long line of hills south of Greenbrier that they call Terrapin Ridge. It always has been one of the best coon-hunting spots in the county, but it's rough country for chasing out-of-season coon hunters in, especially on a dark night. Terrapin Ridge should have been called Rattlesnake Ridge because it is full of these dangerous snakes. Most of the time when I was up in that section on a night-hunting case, I just forgot about the snakes. There wasn't much else you could do.

But one night I was up there checking raccoon hunters, walking through the woods right about at the crest of Terrapin Ridge when suddenly I heard that deadly rattle. It's amazing how loud that damned snake sounded. I froze and stayed that way for twenty minutes before I dared to take a step.

But the hairiest situations I found myself in were caused by people, not the wildlife.

One man I encountered during these first days was walking along Red River shooting fish. He had killed a large bass with a twenty-two rifle and it was a nerve-racking situation because I had had no experience in dealing with a person like this in an adversary situation. In this case it was between the two of us, a one-to-one affair.

"You are under arrest! Turn over your weapon!"

"Go to hell!" He refused to turn over the rifle and when I attempted to take him into custody, he resisted.

I grabbed the rifle and it was a tug-of-war for a while, but finally I twisted it away from him and told him again that he was under arrest. He gave up then completely, but I was terrified, because for the first time in my career as game warden, I was face-to-face with physical violence. But now he was frightened for other reasons. He thought that he was going to jail. I finally got him in the car and under control. (We used pieces of baling wire in those days. Had no handcuffs.) I got him to the county courthouse at Springfield at twelve-fifteen P.M. and I was so impressed with what I had done that I called Judge Earl Swann immediately even though he was then at home and having lunch.

The judge promptly put a chewing on me that I'll never forget.

"I don't try cases between twelve o'clock and one o'clock. My court reopens at one o'clock and don't ever bother me at home or I'll hold you in contempt!"

Well, I managed to hold the fellow until the judge got back from his lunch and we tried the fish shooter. He was found guilty and paid a substantial fine.

In August of 1951, I was working a section of the Red River that parallels the Kentucky-Tennessee state line and I was working it afoot, walking the river, checking on some reports of illegal seining in that section.

I knew from experience that the lawbreakers seined the pools. They walked from pool to pool, but they usually stayed in the river, wading through the rapids. But on the long stretches of rapids, they'd usually come out and walk the shoreline to save time.

I was walking along this old logging road in the middle of the afternoon and when I came to a sharp curve in the road I abruptly met three persons coming my way who were carrying a twenty-foot seine. This of course was a violation of the Tennessee code, and so was that hell of a sackful of fish they were carrying!

When I first saw them, I was about thirty feet away and I stopped because I was so startled.

They stopped. They were surprised, too, but they regained their composure just a little faster than I did. They dropped their seine and the sack of fish right there in the middle of that damn road and took off, running in three different directions.

One of them was a young fellow and unusually tall. He was about six feet six or seven and I guess he weighed about 140 pounds. For some reason, I picked him out to go after. Ordinarily, I select the fattest one in the lot because they are the easiest to run down. You catch the fat ones first, and then concentrate on the others later.

But I picked this tall, thin one and went after him. We crossed the river bottom at a furious rate of speed. Johnson grass was just about waist high here and he was bounding through the stuff like a scared deer. By the time we got to the other side of the bottom, which was, I guess, about a half a mile across, he had a seventy-five-yard lead on me and that boy was putting more distance between us at pretty near every stride.

"That's just about the strongest runner I've ever been up against," I thought to myself. "But we'll see just how tough he is!"

It was completely still that afternoon. The humidity was terrible. It must have been about ninety or ninety-five degrees and it was one hell of a bad day to have to run.

We crossed a fence and went up a hillside, up through an old pasture field. We topped the hill and went down into the valley on the other side and he still showed no sign of tiring.

At that time, I was young and could take it. I really poured it on him, but I still couldn't gain a foot.

We topped the next hill and went down into the next valley and in crossing that valley I at last began to detect some apprehension on his part. He began to look back over his shoulder quite frequently and he fell a couple of times, picking himself up again and sprinting off like a scared rabbit after gaining his second wind.

I had been engaged in foot races with lawbreakers ever since I first pinned on a badge and I had a lot of experience in judging my quarry. Now it was quite apparent to me that this tall young fellow was mine. I knew that I could last longer than he could. I had paced myself to run him to the ground.

We topped the next hill and now I could tell that he was on his last legs because he was staggering and stumbling somewhat, but he was still trying his best to make himself scarce. Once when he turned to look back, I could see that he was freckled-faced and redheaded and about as scared as I have ever seen anybody.

When we reached the top of this last hill, he was still fifty or sixty yards ahead of me. The ridge we were crossing was very abrupt and he dropped out of my sight for nearly a minute before I reached the hilltop myself. On going down the other side, I couldn't see him anywhere. "Well! Where in the hell is he?" I started looking. This was an old hillside pasture field and it had grown up in some briar patches and piles of cedar tops that somebody had cut a long time ago.

Well, hell, he couldn't have gone far because I could see all over that part of the old pasture. "He's hid himself!" I started looking for him and finally found him in a big briar patch. He was curled up there in that briar patch just like a rabbit.

"Come out of there, boy!"

He came out all right, but he came out the other side, his legs moving before he hit the ground. Down this hillside he went. It became apparent that he wasn't going to voluntarily stop and surrender himself to me. I put on an extra burst of speed, caught up to him, and tackled him going down the hill. And this hill was very steep!

I hit him from behind and hit him good, and down we went. We were rolling over and over down this hill and I had no idea who he was or what his reaction would be to this encounter. When we got close to the bottom of the hill, I began to prepare to defend myself against any action he might take. This meant that I had to end up on top by the time we got to the bottom of the hill and I did just this.

I managed to be sitting astraddle of him. He was about two-thirds facedown in the dust. At this point, I identified myself to him as best I could while I was gasping for breath. "I'm—I'm Willie Parker, state conservation officer." I doubt that he could have heard me anyhow, because he was gasping for breath, too; really heaving!

It was apparent that his struggling was going to cause me some trouble, so I got up and eased away from him and prepared to defend myself. But as soon as I got my weight off him, why he just relaxed and lay there, so I sat down beside him while I regained my breath and he regained his.

Then I identified myself again.

"I won't run no more," he said.

"Fine," I answered. "Let's go back to the car."

While we were walking back, I questioned him.

"Who was with you?"

"I don't know."

"What were you doing?"

"Nothin'. I was just walking down that road."

"You were carrying that damn seine!"

"Oh, was I carrying it?"

"You know damn well you were! You were part of the seining party and I'm going to charge you with possessing an illegal fishing device, and I am also going to charge you with refusing inspection by trying to run a game warden to death!"

When we finally got back to the car (we must have run at least a couple of miles), I said, "OK, I want you to set in the car. I'm going to look for your buddies."

I went back down the road to where they had dropped the seine and the sack of fish, and there the fish and the net still were just where they had been dropped. I carried them back to the car, opened up the trunk, and put them in for safekeeping. Then I started after the other two gentlemen.

I started up Red River, walking the shoreline. When I had surprised them, two of them had run straight up the river.

I had proceeded about a thousand yards up the river, I guess, easing along a river edge path. Here the water was reasonably deep. Large, long pools here. I was wondering if I would ever see these two fish poachers again when I noticed a commotion in the water some two hundred yards above me.

Well, anything that causes a ripple when you are looking for anything unusual excites you. Ripples on the surface of an otherwise quiet pool are caused by the actions of something.

I eased up along the bank and I saw that this ripple was coming from under some overhanging roots on the opposite bank. There were some large sycamore trees along the shore. I sat down on my side of the river just where I could get a good view of the ripples that kept coming out from under this overhang and spreading across the pool.

I waited and waited. Was it a muskrat? It could be a fish feeding on the surface. It could have been a fish that had been injured. It could have been most anything, so I just waited to see what would happen.

Then I began to notice muddy water seeping out from under this bank and mingling with the clear water in the pool. "Well! That means that whatever it is, it's a little bit bigger than a fish and it's got to be larger than a muskrat! It just might be a man, this man that I'm looking for!"

So I sat there for about twenty minutes more. Of course, there was an air space under this bank. If it was a man, he wasn't underwater all this time.

Suddenly, I saw some rather frantic movement under there and I saw the hair roots from the trees that were overhanging this bank carefully part. I never will forget the sight of this man sticking his head out of that opening like a damned otter. He looked up the river and he looked down the river, but he never once looked *across* the river to the point where I was sitting. Finally he pulled his head back in.

Well, I picked up a rock about the size of a baseball that was lying on the riverbank and I threw it over there across the river to that overhang. It hit about a foot from where this fellow's head had stuck out.

There was no movement.

I threw another one and then another one and finally his curiosity got the best of him. He began to move, to try to change his position a little bit. But, jammed under the riverbank, he didn't have the room to do that.

I knew he could hear me.

"I'm a state wildlife officer. I have caught your associate and I know who you are, so you just might as well come the hell out from under that riverbank and come on across the river to where I am."

And he came. Swam that damned Red River over to my side. He was a young man.

"Where do you live?"

"I live over at Riverdale."

"Who was the third party? I forgot to spell his name. I didn't have my pencil with me when I ran your buddy down."

And he told me the name of the third one.

I found him, later that afternoon, walking farther up the river.

Anyhow, I cited all three into General Sessions Court at

Springfield, for sometime the following week. They came before Judge Swann down there, and I charged them with taking fish illegally and with refusing inspection by running, which was a violation of the Tennessee code and a statute that I particularly cherished because whenever they ran, it caused me a lot of extra trouble.

The last two I had caught paid their fines: fifty dollars and costs on two counts each, which amounted to over a hundred dollars.

But the third one, the tall, redheaded youth whom I had chased all over the damn countryside, told Judge Swann:

"Well, Jedge, I didn't expect the fine to be that much and I didn't bring that much money with me. Could I walk just across the street to Commerce Union Bank and get a check cashed and I'll bring the money right back over here?"

"Oh," said the judge. "That'll be fine."

I smelled a mouse. "Judge, do you want me to accompany this gentleman over to the bank?"

But Judge Swann shook his head. "Well, Bill, I really don't believe that is necessary. I'm sure that he'll be right back."

"Fine," I said. This was about ten-thirty in the morning. About a quarter to twelve, after court was long adjourned and the judge had gone to his chambers, I finally went around and walked into his office.

"Judge, is it all right if I go over to Commerce Union Bank and find out what the hell it was that took him two hours to cash a check for a hundred and eighteen dollars?" (That was the total cost.)

Judge Swann looked surprised. "Didn't he come back?"

"No," I said. "And I've got a hunch he won't." I went over to the Commerce Union Bank. You could see the bank from the courthouse, so I knew that he would have to go to the bank because he would be apprehensive about us watching him from out the window of the courtroom.

And he had gone to the bank. He went up to a teller in there, as a matter of fact, the assistant cashier, and inquired about the procedure for opening a savings account and after all of this was carefully explained to him, he thanked the cashier and simply walked out.

But he walked out of a side entrance and once he was outside, he flew!

Well, I went back and related all that I had learned to the judge and this infuriated him because he felt that he had gone out of his way to accommodate this fellow by not locking him up because he didn't have the money for the fine in his pocket.

So Judge Swann issued a bench warrant for this tall, skinny redhead whom I had had such a hell of a time catching in the first place.

I took the damned warrant and went right to where this fellow lived on a tenant farm in the northern part of Robertson County and when I got there I was told by his father that he had come in suddenly about eleven-thirty or quarter to twelve. The boy had packed his clothes and gone to Chicago where he planned to seek gainful employment and stay the rest of his life.

Well, violating the Tennessee fishing regulations are petty offenses and they are not offenses where you can extradite a person, so I just marked him off as lost. However, I kept that bench warrant over the sun visor of my car because I had a hunch that Tennessee boys usually have strong home ties and eventually, why, he'd be back sure as hell!

I knew a farmer who lived close to this fellow and I went to see him. "If that long-legged lad comes back here, I want to know it because I've got a warrant for him."

About five months later that farmer did call me. "He's home!"

I made a frantic search for the warrant and found it where I had left it months ago, tucked behind the sun visor.

When I pulled into his lane, I was told by his father, "Yes, he was here. He came in last evening and spent the night here. But now he's joined the army and he's on his way to Fort Hood, Texas."

"How long has he been gone?"

"Well, he's been gone about three and a half hours."

"Where did he leave from?"

"Well, he left from Nashville."

I hurried on down to Nashville and tried to intercept the busload of recruits, but they had already gone by the time I got to Nashville.

So I went back to this farmer-neighbor of the boy's up in north Robertson County.

"I want to know when he gets his first leave because I have a warrant for his arrest and I have some plans for him."

The farmer nodded. "I'll tell you, Bill."

Well, some four months later, the farmer called me again and had one short message for me.

"He's home!"

"That's fine." I legged it up there once again as hard as I could go. There was a long lane that went into the farm where this boy lived and as I drove down that damn lane, I met him coming out.

He was in the custody of a deputy sheriff and two military policemen. He was AWOL from the army. Well, hell, I couldn't very well take him away from the United States Army, so I just told him, "I'll bide my time and I'll see you later."

Well, they carried him away somewhere, but they evidently gave him some sort of a discharge shortly after that, from the rumors I heard.

About a year after the time I first encountered this fellow over on Red River, it was in August on one Sunday afternoon while I was driving through Springfield, I saw him!

Lo and behold, who do I see coming down the sidewalk but this long-legged "stump jumper" that I had been searching for so long. There was a right pretty girl with him and they were holding hands.

I stopped the car as fast as I could and got out, but I was unable to find my warrant. Actually, I could have taken him into custody legally without the damned warrant, so I stepped out on the sidewalk in front of him.

"Hello," I said, "we are still waiting for you to come back from the Commerce Union Bank. There is that matter of one hundred and eighteen dollars you owe the court, and the judge is very distressed at your conduct, and I feel even worse about it than that!"

"Well, Mr. Game Warden," he said, "let me tell you something.

You know I've been to Chicago and you know I've been in the army?"

"Yes," I answered. "I know all that."

"Well," he said, "I've also talked to a lawyer."

"That's great," I said. "What did the lawyer tell you?"

"The lawyer told me that when you and that judge let me walk out of that courthouse, I was footloose and fancy free, and I don't intend to pay you or that court one damned cent!"

"Oh!" I said. "When the lawyer told you that, you got it all straightened out, did you?"

"Yes, I got it all straightened out and besides that, I've just got married. This is my wife."

I nodded to the young lady. "How do you do?"

"And," he said, "I've got me a job down at Clark's ice plant and I'm moving back to Springfield, but I'm not going to pay that fine."

"What shift do you work down there?"

"I work the night shift. I get off at seven o'clock in the morning."

"That's most interesting," I replied. "It's been delightful to see you again and certainly nice to meet your wife. I'll see you later. Good-bye."

So I legged it on down to Judge Swann's house and got another warrant. The next morning at twenty minutes to seven, I pulled up to Clark's Ice and Coal Company.

Well, this "ol' boy" was sitting on the porch of the plant with his head in his hands. He had worked the graveyard shift and he was very tired and sleepy.

When his relief came at seven, he stretched those long legs of his and climbed down off that porch and started walking toward Willow Street.

I pulled up alongside of him in my car.

"Get in and I'll give you a lift."

He looked mighty surprised, but he accepted the offer. "That's mighty nice of you."

"Where do you live?"

"On the other side of town a piece."

We continued on down Willow Street because the jail was at the far end of the street. My passenger looked puzzled. "This ain't the way to my house!"

"No," I said, "but this is the way to the place that you are going to." I showed him the paper. "This is a warrant for your arrest. You are under arrest, so just sit there quietly."

About that time, I pulled up in front of the jail.

That fellow turned white as a sheet. He was very pale. I got out of the car and I led him inside the jailhouse. This was fairly early in the morning and the sheriff who was also the jailer in those days must have still been asleep.

I had this boy in the reception room by that time. I rang the bell on the desk and pretty soon the sheriff came on down.

The sheriff, Otto Murphy, was a friend of mine. "I have a warrant for this man and the court has set bond on the warrant. He has to post bond for an amount of one hundred and twenty-five dollars or we are going to lock him up."

Well, when I mentioned those words, "lock him up," the young fellow became visibly agitated. He started shaking real bad.

The sheriff was still in his night robe. "OK, young man, do you have the amount of the bond?"

"No, I don't have but five dollars on me," he stammered.

The sheriff said, "Well, then you are going to have to come with me. Empty your pockets out on the desk."

The boy emptied his pockets out like he was told to do, but he was getting a right wild look in his eyes.

The bullpen was right behind the jail office, so the sheriff opened the door to the pen and I said to the fellow, "OK, go in there."

"NO!"

"Yes, you go in there!"

He wouldn't budge an inch. "No!"

The sheriff looked at me and winked and I nailed the prisoner on one side while the sheriff grabbed him on the other and we headed him toward the big wide door of the bullpen. I had him by one arm and the sheriff had him by the other. The sheriff was about five nine, I guess, and I was about five seven and a half and this fellow we were dragging was well over six feet, about six feet six. That meant that he was sort of top-heavy and we were dragging an awful lot of him.

As we approached the bullpen, this fellow suddenly reversed himself, swung both legs up in the air, got a foot on either side of that damned door, and kicked back as hard as he could.

When he did, all three of us went ass over teakettle down about seven steps and ended up at the bottom in the biggest mess I had ever seen in my life. We turned over a desk and a chair and I ended up on top of our prisoner and he was raising all kinds of hell.

The sheriff was madder'n hell. "You just hold that son of a bitch there until I get my blackjack and I'll show you how to put him in that bullpen."

I said, "Wait a minute, sheriff. Let's don't hurt him."

The sheriff didn't like the idea very much, but he agreed. "All right, but there ain't nobody gonna get me down in my own damned jail, I'll tell you that for sure."

"Well," I said, "let's just wait a minute." I told the boy I was sitting on, "Look, you're very close to some serious criminal charges. You've assaulted me and you've assaulted the sheriff." Then, all at once, it came out of him in a stream.

He suffered from acute claustrophobia. When he had been in the guardhouse and was confined in a brig, he went completely berserk and that was the basis for his discharge. He just couldn't stand to be confined inside four walls with the door closed. As long as the door was open, he was all right.

Well, after I heard his story, I said, "Look, boy, we've got to do one of two things. You've either got to come up with that bond money or you've got to go to jail and that's all there is to it."

"How much is that bond again?" he asked.

"One hundred and twenty-five dollars."

"Can I make a telephone call?"

"Yes, you can make a telephone call."

Well, he called his grandmother who promptly brought the $125 in cash down there to the jail and carried that young fellow away.

I think that Sheriff Murphy kinda held it against me and I guess if he was still alive, he would to this day. He wanted to mellow that old boy up pretty good and drag him by force into the bullpen.

But, like I said, I always did detest violence.

Sometime around 1952, in June, I got a call one night from a man who wouldn't identify himself, but he sure had one hell of a story to tell.

"Every time it rains," he said, "and the water gets muddy, there is a group of people who take a twenty-foot seine and sweep the north fork of Red River clean of fish.

"The only section of the river they haven't hit so far this year is the section right above Duer's Mill. The next time it rains enough to get the river muddy, if you slip in there you can catch them boys. But be careful, they keep a guard out."

"OK," I replied. "I thank you for the information and I'll go up there after the next rain and I'll be careful."

Well, about four or five days later, it rained about an inch or an inch and a half. I called a farmer I knew who lived at the head of the river.

"George, how about going down to the river and see if it's muddy and rising and if it is, call me back."

In a little while he called me back.

"Hell, I don't know what you've got on your mind, Bill. It's just right. The river's right to seine."

I called Frank Carson who was my supervisor at the time and called another warden, Joel Barnett. "Come on over here and meet me in Greenbrier. I think we can catch us a seining party this afternoon!"

We must have hit the river sometime around one o'clock and we started working it at the Kentucky-Tennessee state line.

We walked a mile and a half or maybe two miles of that river and it was hotter than hell and the horse weed and cane was as high as your head.

Both Frank and Joel got hot. "Bill, how much of this river is in Tennessee?" Joel asked.

"There's about eleven miles of it and we're going to walk every inch of it. Those fellows are going to be on that stream somewhere this afternoon."

We were walking up the river alongside of the bottom. There was a bluff directly across from us, so we were pretty sure they had to come to the river from our side. We crossed a little old road that pulled into the edge of the river and lo and behold, here sets a late model car, pulled back in the cane break and hid.

We left Joel Barnett to watch the car while Frank and I went on up the stream to see if we could encounter the seiners, thinking that they'd be upstream and we'd be behind them.

We walked about a mile and a half from where the car was and we heard noises. We could hear the rather muted sound of excited voices and we knew that we'd found our seining party.

When we got into position where we could see them, they were coming downstream, which we didn't expect. There was one man on the shore and five men in the river, but only two of us, and we knew that we would be in for a hell of a race unless we could pen them in some fashion.

They were then about three hundred yards above us and we decided that we'd let them seine to us and we'd conceal ourselves in the high grass along the creek bank. Frank would take the man on the shore and I would do what I could with the men in the river.

The seiners were catching the fish and they would throw them out onto the bank and the fellow on the bank would pick these fish up and put them in a sack. He had about forty or fifty pounds of mostly smallmouth bass.

They worked their way almost down to where we were hiding and they threw a bass, but that hit about six feet in front of where we were lying real tight, close to the ground.

We could see that fish through the weeds, flopping around some four feet in front of us. This fellow came on down and he reached down to pick up this fish—it was a beautiful smallmouth bass.

Just about the time he got his hands on the flopping fish and pinned the fish to the ground, we raised up on our hands and knees and that son of a bitch was looking us right in the face. There was a look of astonishment and shock on his face. He was trying his best to yell, his mouth was open and his lips were working, but he was so terrified that he wasn't making a sound!

I immediately jumped to my feet and started running to the river just as hard as I could. I had some thirty feet to go to the bank. I thought that I knew the river well. I thought that the bank there was some three or four feet high and I intended to jump from the edge of this bank off into the water. When I got to the edge of the river, I was going full tilt, running at top speed, and when I started to jump, I was already in the air before I realized that the damned bank was some eighteen feet high! I was sailing through the air like a big-assed bird and came down right in the middle of that damned river. I hit the water, which was just about up to my neck. Of course, I went under and while I was under that water, I drew my pistol. I never will forget the water running out of its muzzle as I came up.

There was a son of a bitch there in the water beside me with a sycamore "rousting" pole about eight feet long and he took a cut at my head with that damned pole.

The water was still running out of the end of that pistol barrel when I said, "Drop that pole or I'll hurt you." He laid the pole down. I had that bunch cold.

"OK, gentlemen, just walk up the bank there and sit down on the log."

They lined up on the old driftwood log like a bunch of damned turtles sunning themselves.

We marched them down to the car where Joel was waiting and wrote them up.

chapter 5

The Dangers
of the Job

IT WAS DURING the early fifties, after I had been working as a game warden in Robertson County, Tennessee, for a couple of years and had made my presence known, that the outlaw element began to ferociously resist my efforts to enforce the laws relating to the protection of our wildlife.

They did this in many ways. They would pull the water hoses off my car and throw them away, they let the air out of my tires, and sometimes even slashed them. I received threatening telephone calls, but they never actually tried to harm me in person.

It was evident that they were trying to intimidate me in some manner, but in the fall of 1951, things began to get more serious. I received a telephone call about a quarter to two on one Sunday morning. This in itself wasn't anything unusual because I got telephone calls twenty-four hours a day and I responded to every one of them.

This time when I picked up the phone, a well-modulated voice asked, "Is this Mr. Parker?"

"Yes, it is."

"Are you the conservation officer?"

"Yes, I am."

The voice on the other end of the line then said, "Well, you are a common son of a bitch!"

I replied, "Oh? I wasn't aware of that!"

"Well, you are and let me tell you. If you ever come into the Barren Plains area of Robertson County ever again, we are going to kill you!"

I said, "Evidently I am talking to a very bad man."

"You're damn right you are!"

"Well, if you are as bad as you seem to think you are, why don't you tell me who you are and where you are and I will come to see you right away. It is apparent that we have a difference and it needs to be resolved."

"What kind of a damn fool do you think I am?"

"Well," I answered, "I don't want to discuss that at this time of night. I just want to know who you are and where you are."

The voice on the phone answered, "I'm not going to tell you who I am and I'm not going to tell you where I am. I'm simply going to tell you this. If you don't stay out of the Barren Plains section, you are going to get killed." (This was an area that was notorious for fish gigging on the Red River.)

I said, "OK, I appreciate the information and I consider this a threat and I will probably see you within the next twenty-four hours."

Well, this stunned him. "What do you mean the next twenty-four hours?" He hung up abruptly.

When he was talking on the phone, I could hear, in the background, honky-tonk music and a lot of talking going on and I knew damn well that the call was local. I also knew that there was just one place in Robertson County that sold beer (Robertson County was dry; you couldn't buy whiskey there) and would be open after midnight. This place would permit its beer-drinking customers to buy up a whole bunch of bottles, set them on the tables where they could stay until three or four o'clock in the morning and drink. The owner of Old Cedar Place didn't seem to care or worry about the sheriff and it was common knowledge throughout Robertson County that even though the doors closed here at twelve midnight, the drinking continued.

Well, hell, I promptly dressed. This nightclub was just exactly seven miles from my home, so it didn't take me long to get in my car and drive out there. It was closed, as I knew it would be. The front door was locked and so was the back door. But I could hear a whole bunch of stuff going on inside the place. There was laughing and talking and loud music and it was apparent that there was a good-sized crowd inside.

I pounded on the door until the proprietor came to the door and, of course, he knew me. I said, "Jim, I want to come in and talk with you."

"Come on in. No one with you?"

"No, I'm alone."

When I got inside, there were a couple of dozen men there. There was a long bar around this place and they sold barbecue and beer, but mostly beer.

I said, "Jim, I got a telephone call about twenty-five minutes ago that had to come from this place. Now there is only one telephone in this damn place and it's right there on the wall. It's a public telephone and it's impossible for anyone to use it without you knowing it. Now who in the hell used that telephone about twenty-five minutes ago?"

"Well," he said, "I don't know."

"Oh, yes you do know." I looked at my watch. "You also know that it's well into Sunday morning and I can see at least fifty bottles on the tables. Some of them look like they are full and everyone is drinking. Now, who in the hell used that telephone?"

"Man," he said, "I hate to do this. What are you planning to do?"

"Nothing. I just want to go see him."

"You're not going to hurt him?"

"I don't have any intentions of hurting anybody and I also don't have any intentions of getting hurt. I want to know who made that damned call."

"Well, it was Tom Ellsworth."

"Did you hear any of the conversation?"

"Is this going to end up in court?"

"Well," I answered, "I don't know where it will end up. But I want to know what he said before he called and what he said after he called."

"Well, Bill, I'm going to tell you the truth. It seems like he made some threats before he called, but I couldn't swear to that. It's funny though. Right after he hung up that phone, he paid his tab and he left. He looked worried."

I said, "OK, that's fine. I appreciate this no end and I hope you have a nice day."

So I left. I went home and went back to bed. The next morning, I got up and drove straight to this man's house. He lived on a farm that his father owned up near Barren Plains. He was about twenty-eight years old, a typical country boy who had never been out of blue denims and didn't know what a game law was.

I knew his father, old man John Ellsworth, well and asked him which of the two or three houses on his farm was where this son lived.

"Bill, is something wrong?"

"I don't think so," I said. "I've just got a little something that I've got to get settled with Tom, but I think I can handle it."

The old farmer looked worried. "Well, is it serious?"

"I don't think so. I don't think you need to be concerned about it. I'll stop by on my way back." So I went on down the lane, walked up on his porch, and knocked on the door. This ol' boy came to the door himself and it was quite apparent that he'd had a long night and that he had bent that right elbow many times during that night. His eyes were red, he'd been sleeping off one hell of a drunk. It was a good time to hit him.

I didn't carry a gun because, you see, I had to build an image in Robertson County and let these lawbreakers know that I wasn't afraid of them and held them in contempt. If I had gone to that house obviously armed, that might have been prudent. But if I walked in there with my bare ass hanging out, right into his own place, then this would psychologically intimidate him in a sense.

He came to the door. "Hello, Mr. Parker."

"I would like to see you a minute, please."

"Would you like to come inside?"

"No, I would prefer that you come outside."

He looked worried, maybe even a little scared. "Are we going to have trouble?"

"I don't think so, I don't think so," I answered. "I just want to talk with you."

"OK, I'll be out in a minute."

Well, I walked out into the front yard and I waited and just about the time it would take for a man to get dressed, he came on out.

"I came to talk to you about your telephone call this morning."

"I didn't call you, Mr. Parker."

I said, "Look, let me put it on the line. You called and I can prove you called. Now I came to talk to you about your telephone call this morning. What you did is a violation of laws that I don't enforce. It is a serious violation of the Tennessee code to threaten a state officer and that is precisely what you did. You did it in an anonymous fashion, but I can tie that call to you without any doubt.

"I want to explain to you what I am trying to do and why I am trying to do it and why I am not awed by you or by anyone else. I intend to control the actions of the illegal hunters and fishermen in this county. I need help. I don't need enemies and I don't need you for an enemy. But I want you to thoroughly understand that I am not frightened by you and I wouldn't be if all of your neighbors were standing here in this yard with you.

"If anything happened to me, and I don't think that it will, the state would simply hire someone else to take my place and do exactly what I am doing. There is no way you can kill them all, so the smartest thing that you can do is to join me."

Well, this sermon put this young man, who had threatened my life, in a sort of state of shock. He had expected me to come out there and say, "OK, you common son of a bitch, you called me up and threatened me and now I'm going to whip the hell out of you right here in your own damn yard. I'm going to put you under arrest for threatening the life of a state officer."

He shook his head, as bewildered as if I had connected a hard right to his damn jaw. "Bill, you make me feel like a dog."

"I tried to," I answered.

"Well, I was drinking last night and I've been pissed off ever since you caught them Justin boys down there."

"Why did you get pissed off about that?"

"You didn't treat them fair. You threatened them."

I said, "That's right. I had to protect myself. One of them Justin boys threatened to use a gig on me. I told him if he didn't lay it down, I would kill him. He laid it down and I didn't have to kill him."

The winter months in Robertson County, during the early fifties, were unbelievably cold. There was a period of time then that extended through October, November, and December when the streams would become crystal clear and you could see a dime on the bottom of a pool that was fifteen feet deep. This situation made the fish highly vulnerable because the water was not only clear but also extremely cold and the fish were in a semidormant state.

Some of the people up there in the northern section of Robertson County had learned that their hooded gasoline lanterns could cast a ray of light that would penetrate those clear-water pools all the way to the bottom where the fish lay. They could work their boats over these huge holes at night, spearing fish with ease. These were select game fish. The Red River is a cold-water mountain stream that comes out of Kentucky and into Tennessee. It was then well populated with smallmouth bass, and walleye pike, not to mention a hell of a lot of lesser fish. It was one hell of a stream, but it was, in the forties and fifties, badly abused by the fish giggers.

When I worked this river in the cold months, looking for small-game violators, I would notice signs of fish gigging. I would see where boats had been put in and taken out of the river, and I would also find a fish here and there that had been hit with a gig and wounded but not impaled on the long barbed prongs that were razor sharp.

There had been some grumblings in the north-central section of the county to the effect that "we're going to spear fish and nobody is going to stop us and if anybody does try to stop us, well, they'll get hurt."

Some of the reputable people up in this area were really concerned about my safety. "Bill, never come up here at night after the giggers without bringing the sheriff or a state patrolman with you. It's a bad, a dangerous situation."

I thought about this a lot but decided that if I went into this thing with help, the giggers would think, "That young punk has to hide behind the skirts of the sheriff. He can't take the bad ones alone."

So I worked Red River alone. I spent twenty-one cold nights sitting on a bluff overlooking Red River several miles below Keysburg. There was a stretch of river there that had a fine section of fishing water on it and I knew that these people, about whom I had been getting reports, would have to hit that hole of water sooner or later.

There is, in this section of Red River, a series of deep holes; some of the pools might be as much as fifteen or twenty feet deep. Of course I didn't pay much attention to those deeper pools because there weren't too many gigs with handles over twelve feet. I did see a gig with a fifteen-foot handle on it once, but that was an exception.

But most of this water was right for normal gigging operations. There would be rapids, then a pool, and then more rapids. Some of these holes were a mile and a half long of beautiful water. So I sat there on my bluff and waited—waited damn near a whole month of cold nights.

It was about eight o'clock on the twenty-first night that I saw the light. They had come into view from the river above me and they were on a relatively long stretch of water, probably a quarter of a mile long.

I watched them through binoculars. There were two people in a flat-bottomed boat and I figured, "Well, these must be the two tough-talking Justin brothers."

They were paddling the boat and every once in a while one of them would strike through the water with his gig. They were having remarkable success. I could see that there was quite a pile of fish in the bottom of the boat.

The problem was, I didn't know where they would take out. It became apparent by watching them that they were getting ready to leave the river soon and that it would probably be on the side opposite the one where I was stationed. My side was all steep bluff, making it impossible to pull a boat out of the water.

I had to get across that river! So I went down to a lower ripple (it was about seventeen degrees above zero that night), took off all my clothes, and waded that damn river several hundred yards below the giggers. I thought, "Wouldn't I be in one hell of a mess if they caught me here in the middle of the river stark naked and half frozen like the fish! I would be an easy target for their damn gig."

Once I got on the other side, I put all my clothes back on and came up the river. I knew that they would take out at a spot very close to where I was waiting. I had been concerned about the threats that I had heard and on this particular night, I carried a shotgun loaded with buckshot. It was one of the few times in my career that I ever carried a long gun.

When they came out, they came down through a ripple and pulled their boat up on a sandbar. I was concealed right at the edge of the bank by that sandbar. I let them get out of the boat so that there would be no chance for them to push the boat out again and escape over the rapids that I had just crossed.

They stepped out of the boat and set their lantern down. I think that they were planning to build a fire. I could tell that they were as cold as hell. It was a very cold night and I'd had about all of the waiting around in it that I wanted.

I stepped out from the bank and put my light on them. "State conservation officer! Stand where you are!" I was close to them. Just a few feet between us.

A fish gig makes a formidable weapon. This one had six-inch tines on it, four razor-sharp tines with barbs. They looked bad. They were bad. A devil's weapon. I could imagine how one would feel imbedded in your flesh.

I didn't intend to face that gig this night. When I threw the light on them, one of the boys stepped to the front of the boat, grabbed the gig, and raised it like a spear.

"You may throw it," I told him, "but you'll never live to see it hit! LAY IT DOWN!" I had the shotgun barrel poked out in front of my flashlight where he could see it and he did. He dropped the gig.

"Now step back away from it!" He did.

I eased around with my gun still on them, picked the gig up and broke its damned handle out, and pitched it over next to the bank. Then I sat them down on the bow of the boat. I never got too close because they were surly as hell.

"I want some information from you."

After getting the information I needed, I took their gig, I took their lantern, and I took their fish. I was afraid to take their boat because I was alone and I knew that if I got to fooling around with that damn boat, I would be vulnerable to an attack. In fact, I wasn't able to take all of the fish. I took only the game fish and left the rough fish in the boat.

"Now you fellows are free to go. But leave the boat exactly where it is. I'll be back for it in the morning."

I got out. I brought their lantern and gig with me, went to my car, and went home.

The next morning, I got apprehensive about going back up there. One of the Justin boys lived over in Kentucky and he had a pretty bad reputation. So I first went back to the bluff and checked with my glasses. If they were waiting for me at the boat, I would know it and take whatever action I thought was necessary.

But the boat was gone, and the fish were gone!

They came into court and entered a plea of guilty. (I had only charged them with taking fish illegally.) But they were hostile as hell. They were mad and they were going to stay mad.

Maybe it was about a month after this that I was patrolling the area in which they lived, right on the Kentucky-Tennessee line, and slipped off a dirt road, right into a ditch.

It's a hell of a job getting a car out of a ditch by yourself. I was trying to jack it up and put a log under the wheel and then jack it up again and repeat the operation until I was clear out of the ditch. It meant several hours of damn hard and dirty work.

Well, all of a sudden, I noticed that this same boy who had

threatened me with the gig was coming down the road in an old farm truck. As he went by, and then slowed down and started backing up, I thought, "Oh, hell, here we go!"

He got out of the truck and came over to where I was. "You in trouble?"

"Yes, I am. I slipped off the damn road."

"Well, I got a chain on this old truck. Want me to pull you out?"

I said, "It sure would beat jacking this thing up and building up with logs, if you would."

He nodded and went back to the truck, backed it down to where I was stuck, and got out a logging chain. He hooked it to the front of the old car I was driving at the time—I think it was a 1933 Ford coupe—and he pulled me back on the road.

"I really appreciate this," I said. "It would have taken me at least two hours of hard work to get that car back on the road."

"Well, I've been thinking about calling you." He was a big, well-built fellow and he shuffled his heavy work shoes in the dust of the road as he spoke.

"Well, I got a phone. Anytime I can be of help, I'll be glad to."

"You know," he finally said, "we got awful mad over that thing down on the river that night."

"I know you did. That was a very bad situation that night and I think the whole thing was caused by a bunch of loose talk in the town. I don't think that either of you boys were really planning to hurt me."

He grinned. "There was no way! We wouldn't have hurt you, but if there had been any 'rabbit' in you, we sure as hell would have put you up over the bank! Hell, Bill, that fish gigging is just about the only sport we have. We ain't never going to give it up without a fight. You know that."

One of the Tennessee Thanksgiving traditions was an early morning hunt in which the entire family, including the uncles and cousins, took part to work up an appetite, I imagine for that big dinner.

This was a bad day for gross overlimit violations because this was the first day the rabbits and quail had been shot at and they didn't have that wary quality that was developed after that first day of damned hard shooting. We usually hit the fields on Thanksgiving morning by dawn and we would stay with it until dark. In the course of the day we would check some two or three hundred hunters with a couple of us wardens working together.

On this particular Thanksgiving Day in the early fifties, Ed Gibbs and I were working together near the Kentucky-Tennessee state line near Adams, Tennessee.

About nine-thirty in the morning we heard some shooting and some dogs running across the hill from us. We walked across the hillside. It was a lovely late November morning, not too warm. We had on wool shirts, hunting pants, leather boots; had our side arms strapped on.

We walked across the crest of this hill and we saw four people out in this field only about fifty feet from us. Running from the game warden in Tennessee was a standard damn practice then. It always tickled me to death to see one of those hunters run, because when you put a "hurtin' " on him on his own ground and ran him down, it kinda added to your reputation, a reputation the Game Commission badly needed in Tennessee at that time.

We started toward this small group of hunters and one broke and ran. I mean he took off like a striped ass. He was really moving! I took off behind him. The secret to running people down is, you don't spurt and exhaust yourself within the first three or four or five minutes because that's precisely what they are doing. You kinda just take up a comfortable stride and you just stay with it because he's carrying a shotgun and you're not. He's frightened and you're not. He's going to burn himself out pretty quick. He's going to get tired and then he'll be simple to catch.

Well, I chased this one at a pretty good pace and was gaining on him and he kept looking back. The other three hunters stood and, of course, Ed went to check them.

I pinned this young fellow in a fence corner about a quarter of a mile from where the chase had started. It was an old rail fence corner and when he ran into it, he was aware that as close as I was, he couldn't get over that damned fence before I could get my hands on him.

He whirled. I was some fifteen feet away from him and he threw that shotgun right in my face. I saw his finger move. It was an old twelve-gauge Remington Model-11. I saw him when he kicked the safety off.

I froze.

He was gibbering, nothing that he was saying could I understand. He was frothing at the damned mouth, and it absolutely terrified me.

I stood there.

I tried to calm him, tried to talk to him.

"Why don't you just lay that gun down, son?"

Hell, I wasn't getting through to him at all. There was no way. I decided I'd better get the hell away from him because he was going to shoot. It was just a matter of time. He was going to shoot!

That damned shotgun had about a thirty-inch barrel on it and I knew what kind of a job that shotgun would do to me at fifteen or twenty feet.

I was very careful not to put my hand close to my side arm and I watched him, trying to calm him, talked to him just as soothing as I could.

He was the wildest individual I have ever seen in my life. He appeared to have difficulty in focusing his eyes. He was ranting and raving like a madman. I thought, "Hell, I have never encountered a situation like this."

He had got tired holding the gun and had lowered it. At least he had dropped the muzzle away from the upper part of my body.

I decided, "I'll get the hell away from this son of a bitch. He must be as crazy as a loon!" I took three steps backward and up that gun came and I'm telling you he was serious. I froze again.

"What the hell am I going to do?" I thought. "I can't crowd him and I can't back up!"

When you get caught in that position, you have to take your

chances. There's no way out. They say you can taste fear. I know precisely what it tastes like.

I was only about twenty-five years old at this time. My only chance was for Ed Gibbs to come.

He did come over the hill, but he came from another direction. He had gone down to check another hunter before he came to find out what the hell was keeping me so long.

I could see him from the corner of my eye. When he got about fifty yards away I said softly, "Hold it, Ed." He stopped.

My attention went back to the boy holding the shotgun on me.

"Now, friend, there's two of us. Lay your gun down. We just want to talk to you."

He went into another damned frenzy. Cursing, screaming, but that gun was right smack on my face.

I decided then that we were going to have to hurt him.

I told Ed, "Step away from him. Get to one side of him and when I give the word, you know what to do."

Then I heard a noise behind me and I was afraid to turn and look. Finally an old man came to my view on the right-hand side and he said, "Son, lay the gun down."

It was the boy's father. He turned the gun on his father and started the same ranting and raving, completely unintelligible.

"We're going to have to take him, mister!"

The old man looked at me. "For God sake, don't. Don't try or he'll shoot for sure."

The gun went from me to his father—from his father to me—from me to his father.

I had shut up. I had decided that his father would have more influence on him than I would. His father kept talking to him and trying to get close to him. The boy kept waving that gun back and forth from one of us, then the other. The old man worked himself in to about ten steps from that boy when suddenly the boy turned and raised the gun over his head as high as he could raise it.

He threw it on the ground and then collapsed in the damndest emotional display! He was tearing up chunks of sedge grass. He was screaming and raving. When that gun hit the ground, it exploded and the grass and dirt flew everywhere. The gun hadn't stopped recoiling before I had both my feet on that damned thing.

In the meantime, the other two boys had come up and it took all of us to subdue this fellow rolling around on the ground. We finally got him to his feet and his old man and three brothers took him on to the house.

I looked at my partner.

"Ed, what the hell is wrong?"

"Bill, that boy has been in the Western Kentucky State Hospital for the Insane for six years. They thought that he was well enough to come home for Thanksgiving and he insisted on going hunting, and they let him go with them!"

You never knew what to expect over the next hilltop, but damned if sometimes I don't believe that those rabbit hunters I encountered in the early days were the most dangerous game law violators of them all!

It was sometime during 1950–51 that I was working one Sunday afternoon over on Sycamore Creek, along the Cheatham-Robertson county line, making a routine patrol for closed-season small game hunting.

This was early in November. I got on top of a hill over there in that rough, backwoods country and I could hear some dogs running. I listened to the hounds baying and from that I knew they were beagle hounds. Shortly, I heard a shot. I started moving in the direction of the shooting on foot. It was coming from the south side of Sycamore Creek. Well, the south side of the creek was in Cheatham County and I wasn't assigned to that county, but I had a statewide authority so I went on over, found a rifle, and waded the creek.

It was a lovely autumn day. When I got on the other side, I walked up a hillside and down through a valley into an area of old pasture fields that had grown up into thickets, old briar patches, and what have you, and I got in a good position to see and I thought, "Well, hell's fire!" I think that there were nine people strung out across that hillside, rabbit hunting and the season still closed.

"Hell, I'll get what I can!" I thought. I knew they were going to run. They were bad to run in those days and I was pretty good at running myself, but hell, I couldn't run in nine different directions at the same time!

I walked to the closest one. They were in a kind of scraggly line and the closest one was some thirty-five feet from me and the minute I walked out, he threw a twelve-gauge shotgun right in my face.

"State wildlife officer!" I said. "You fellows hold it!"

The man with the shotgun, dressed in bib overalls and a little on the old side, maybe about sixty, yelled, "RUN, boys! I got 'im!"

He told me, "Don't move, I'll kill ye!"

I stood of course. I stood there and watched the other eight run away with the damn dogs going with them. They had the rabbits hanging on their belts, and the man who had the shotgun on me had two or three rabbits hanging on him. I didn't move because a shotgun at that range is an extraordinarily dangerous and deadly device and it doesn't make a damn what kind of shot or load he's got in the chamber. At that range of about thirty feet it'll kill you and I knew it. I also knew damn well that there was no way that I could draw my thirty-eight pistol and lay him down prior to the time he could pull the trigger.

I had always used the philosophy that I could control just such a situation through talk rather than trying to harm another human being. I stood there.

"Turn around and get the hell off of my place!"

When he said that I knew who he was. I called him by name. "Radnor, I'm not going to leave your place."

"You're gonna get hurt!" he replied.

"That's quite possible, that's quite possible, but I don't think so. I'm not going to leave your place. I'm here on official business and there's certain things that I have to do. I know who you are and I know who those people are that ran. The rabbit season is closed and you are violating state game laws and you know it. You are also violating a more serious law by holding that shotgun on me. I didn't come here to hurt you or anybody else, but I didn't come here to get hurt either. I want you to lay the shotgun down."

He said, "Hell no!"

This was a damned old single barrel that cocked on the side. It didn't have the regular hammer. I don't recall who made those guns. I've seen less than a dozen of them in my entire life. I knew the gun was cocked because I'd seen him latch that hammer down.

He still had that gun up. I took two or three steps toward him.

He swung his gun until it was bearing smack on my face. "Don't come a step closer or I'll kill you!"

"Lay the gun down!"

"No!"

"Lay the damn gun down. I'm not going to leave here. I'm going to take you."

I was actually afraid to turn and leave. I had made a mistake when I told him that I knew who he was. I was afraid to turn and walk away from him because he was trembling like a damned leaf and he was madder'n a damned hornet and he was on his own place and at that time, when a game warden came on a place in that rough section of the state, he was considered an intruder.

Well, I maneuvered myself for over a period of about thirty minutes. You can't hold a shotgun up in a threatening position forever. He finally just had to lower it. He had to lower it down. His arms got to shaking.

I'd take a couple of steps.

He'd bring that damned shotgun back up.

I finally worked myself in to where I was about six or eight feet from him. He had the gun on me.

I stopped. "Look, lay the gun down. Let's sit down and talk this out. I'll take this damned pistol off and pitch it up there in that thicket."

He seemed frozen—as if he were in a trance—but I could tell he was getting himself worked up to the point where I thought he was going to do something fast, so I hit him. I grabbed that gun by the barrel, tried to get the hammer, but it was too late. The gun went off right up in the air close to my face. I felt the surge of heat when the load went up through the barrel.

And I threw that old man right smack on his ass in a briar patch. When he came up, he came up with a knife in his hand. When he came up with that damned switchblade, I pulled my thirty-eight.

"Fold 'er up and put it back in your pocket."

He folded that knife up.

"Sit down, now."

He sat down.

I said, "Now look. You are a damned fool. You've committed a felony by pulling that damned shotgun on me. Now what's your problem?"

"I just don't want you on my land."

"Look, mister, I'm a state officer enforcing a state law. I have every right to be on your property."

"Are you going to take me in?"

It was getting late by this time. It was rather late in the afternoon when I got into this place.

"No," I replied, "I don't think I will. I really don't think I will. Those were your boys that ran?"

"That's right."

"Well, I tell you what I'm going to do. I'm going back home tonight, but I'm coming to your house in the morning. I know where you live. I'm going to take you and those five boys of yours who are eighteen or over and can be prosecuted, over before a Cheatham County magistrate and I'm going to file charges against all six of you for hunting during a closed season. I don't think that I'll go before the grand jury for an indictment on the assault charge. I think I know how you feel. What I want to do is to try to impress upon you and your family and your neighbors that I intend to enforce these damned game laws."

He looked at me like he couldn't believe what he was hearing.

"You mean you are not going before the grand jury on that shotgun deal?"

"No, this time, I'm not. But let me tell you that what you did was very dangerous. You didn't know what I was going to do. We both could have been lying dead in this damned field by now."

"Yes," he said. "That's sure right."

"All right. Now take the rabbits off your belt. I want you to give me your word that you'll be ready to go at eight o'clock and that you'll have those boys there with you."

"I give you my word. Are you going to take my shotgun?"

"No." I handed the damned gun back to this man. He stood there and looked at me and I could see both surprise and respect in his eyes.

"Okay, I'll see you in the morning about eight o'clock."

I turned my back to him and walked away. Cold chills ran up my spine, but I had to do this. I had to show him that I had nothing but contempt for his actions or what he might do. After I got to the edge of the woods and looked back, he was still standing there with the gun in his hand and it was broke down.

When I got on top of that damned hill, I trembled like a leaf because this man had a bad reputation in the community as a dangerous man.

The next morning it was colder than hell and there was quite a frost on the ground. I came tooling down that backcountry dirt road in the 1933 Ford coupe and pulled up to his house. This was an old roughhouse setting in Sycamore Hollow. A great big frame house. It had never been painted.

You don't pull up in front of those houses in the backcountry and blow a damned horn. You get out and you holler.

There was blue smoke coming out of that chimney and there was heavy frost everywhere, and there was an old pickup and a jeep and rusty farm machinery in the yard, and three or four coon dogs and a dozen beagle hounds.

I got out of the car, left my gun on the seat, walked up to the porch, and yelled "HELLO!"

The door opened. A young lad about thirteen or fourteen came out on the porch.

"Are you Mr. Parker?"

"Yes, I am."

"My dad says to come on in."

I walked in. They were back in the kitchen at this big, long rough board table eating breakfast.

Les got up. "Good morning, Mr. Parker. Have you had your breakfast?"

"Yes, I have."

"Would you like coffee?"

"Yes, I would. Very much."

That table was loaded down with good country eating. Home-cured ham and sausage, homemade bread, scrambled eggs, the works. All of his boys were there, and they were all "hosses."

After breakfast, the man I had come after said, "Mr. Parker, are you ready to go?"

"Yes, I am."

We walked out in the yard and took one look at my car.

"We all can't get in that car."

"That's right! I never thought of that. We'll either have to make a couple of trips out of it or you'll have to drive one of your vehicles in."

"I'm going to take the jeep. You take two of the boys with you."

He loaded the other three boys who were of legal age into the jeep and that damned jeep didn't even have doors on it and it was colder'n hell.

We went on down the Sycamore Creek road, on into Pleasant View to the nearest magistrate and we held court.

There were six of them. Five boys and the old man. The magistrate asked what I was charging them with and I told him, "Hunting rabbits during the closed season."

"What's the fine on that?" the magistrate asked.

"It runs from twenty-five to fifty dollars."

"What's your recommendation, Warden?"

"The minimum fine and the costs."

"All right. Let me ask you something. Did these people give you any trouble, Mr. Parker?"

"I had a little trouble with Mr. Radnor, but we settled it out in the field."

"Well," the magistrate said, "I'm glad of that because we ain't going to put up with no people getting funny with the game wardens here!"

The fines amounted to twenty-nine dollars and seventy-five cents each, and there wasn't that much money in that part of the damned county.

The rabbit hunters could come up with all of it but forty dollars.

"Mr. Magistrate, would it be all right if I brought the balance over here to you tomorrow?"

The magistrate shook his head. "I usually make 'em pay up before they leave."

"Judge," I said. "This man here is as good as his word. If you let him do that, I'll appreciate it."

The magistrate agreed and those people went on home, wiser men.

I had learned something, too, even if I damned near did get my head blown off. You got to stand up to these people.

It was real early in the game that I learned that as long as I was a 125-pound game warden and measured about five feet seven, I had to use my wits instead of my weight if I was to stay alive.

chapter 6

Undercover Work
in Tennessee

REELFOOT LAKE LIES in the shape of a human embryo, curled against itself in the far western corner of Tennessee where the state meets both Kentucky and Missouri. According to an old Indian legend, the lake was named after an Indian hunter who ran with a peculiar side-winding gait that gave him the name of Reelfoot.

Reelfoot fell in love with the beautiful daughter of a fierce Indian chieftain. The girl, so beautiful that she blinded the eyes of the strongest of men, was aptly named Starlight.

Reelfoot asked for Starlight as his wife and was refused in no uncertain terms. One night, Reelfoot and Starlight crept off in the forest together and the wrath of the powerful Indian chieftain fell not only upon this brash young warrior who stole his daughter, but on the countryside as well.

Hence, Reelfoot Lake was named, but its birth was one of the great labor pangs and upheavals of Mother Nature herself.

While on an undercover assignment, I was exposed to this famous lake for three years. Without question it is the most fantastically beautiful spot on this earth.

Reelfoot Lake was formed in 1811 by a violent earthquake that must have been felt over a wide section of the middle United States. The lake is situated on the alluvial plains of the Mississippi River in Lake and Obion counties, Tennessee. As a result of the earthquake, a vast area of virgin forest sunk and the Mississippi River actually flowed backward to form Reelfoot. There are old tales from people of the area who remembered those shocks and the fear and suffering the earthquake caused.

But, it was almost as if Nature were paying mankind back for the devastation she had wreaked on the area. At first Reelfoot was a vast lake, beautiful clear water with some of the original cypress trees lining its shore. While some virgin cypress still remains, other younger trees have grown, etching the shoreline of Reelfoot with deep mysterious shadows of dense growth of trees and underbrush. You can't visit the lake without a strange feeling of reverence and awe.

The lake itself is so fertile that it produces a great amount of food for fish and wildlife. Since its formation in 1811, great flights of migratory waterfowl have made this their winter home and beginning some twenty years ago, Reelfoot became the most important wintering ground for the southern bald eagle. These great birds seem to reign over the lake during the winter months when we have recently counted populations of as many as 175 birds.

Reelfoot is the type of area where you can see almost any form of fish or wildlife that's indigenous to Tennessee, as well as many species of plants.

But the deepest impression you get of this lake is its overall beauty. It can be termed a natural lake, but every time I view it, there is always in the back of my mind the great force that must have been generated when Reelfoot Lake was formed. Now much of the lake has reverted to swamp, a deep swamp. Some of the lake will eventually revert back to dry land as it once was. There is a very serious silt problem here and one man-made drainage canal has been constructed to control the water level of this unusual lake.

Conservationists are trying to control and prolong the life of Reelfoot as long as possible. But the lake has a history of lawlessness that, until recent years, goes back to its beginning. The great amount and variety of wildlife and fish that made Reelfoot Lake and the surrounding area its home, also attracted poachers and market hunters from wide, a three-state area of Tennessee, Missouri, and Kentucky.

Prior to the opening of the 1953 hunting season, I was called to Nashville headquarters of the Tennessee Game and Fish Department and attended a meeting with Fred Williams, state law enforcement chief, and Boots Hammonds, agent in charge of Tennessee for the United States Fish and Wildlife Service.

These men related to me that they were having trouble, a serious problem in west Tennessee and primarily around Reelfoot Lake with the market hunting of waterfowl. They said that the thing there was just about out of control and that they had made extensive plans to put teams of undercover agents in the area to see what intelligence they could derive from the local people. These agents were to pose as wealthy hunters.

This all sounded pretty exciting to me. I agreed to be a part of the program and I learned that John Drennan, conservation officer for Wilson County, would work with me.

John was a happy-go-lucky sort of fellow, older than I. He was about forty-four at the time and had just completed auctioneering school, a profession in which he was much interested. He had also just begun to practice on a duck call.

The beginning of the assignment was anything but undercover. All the way from Middletown to Reelfoot Lake in the western corner of Tennessee, John insisted on practicing being an auctioneer. "All right now, folks ... What am ah bid on this heah item ... ? Do ah heah a dollah, a dollah and a half, half half?" His singsong chant would fill the car and then he'd switch over to practicing with that damn duck call. It was cold and the car was closed. A duck call in such tight quarters will split your head wide open.

We finally arrived at Samburg, Tennessee, a little village on Reelfoot Lake, and checked into Hutchcraft's Motel. The man who at that time was the operator of the motel was one of our prime targets. We made his acquaintance and chartered him as a guide.

We hunted for three days down there. We'd run over the lake all day and usually kill our limit of birds. The guide, Jim Hutchcraft, was very cordial and so finally we propositioned him on the matter of selling us a few ducks.

"No, sir! Uh, uh! I don't know nothin' about selling ducks." He wasn't about to sell us any ducks.

Well, we came on back to headquarters and we stayed home for about a week and then we went on down for another three-day hunting trip.

At the end of this trip, we again approached the guide. "How about selling us a few ducks to take back?" During this period we had seen a large number of ducks being loaded into expensive automobiles with Illinois and Missouri license plates on them and we were sure those ducks were being sold.

But we were unable to buy a thing. Not one damned duck! It was a baffling situation. We approached this man again after hunting with him for six days.

"No! Hell no, I'm not going to sell you any ducks. Look, you fellows are professional men, businessmen and evidently you've got plenty of money. You come here to have a good time. You go out and hunt all day. You come back to the motel and you just set in your room. You don't do any honky-tonkin', you don't run out, you don't drink, you don't do one damn thing at night but just set in your room.

"When a man comes down here and acts like you fellows acting, it's either one of two things. He's either a preacher or a damned game warden and down here we don't have much time or use fer either one!"

"Well, it's just strange country, you know," we assured him that we were neither preacher nor game warden, that we were just kind of getting the feel of things before we cut loose. "We're reputable business people, and we certainly don't want to get involved in any kind of trouble, you know."

We went back to Nashville and related our experiences with this man at Reelfoot to Boots Hammonds and Fred Williams, and decided to play our parts a little more realistically. We began buying whiskey and taking it back to Reelfoot Lake with us on these trips.

We were posing as tobacco men out of Bowling Green, Kentucky. We had a pretty good setup. They checked on us several times. We had a telephone number of someone we knew would work with us, but a phony address where we couldn't be reached.

Well, anyhow, about the third or fourth trip out with this guide from Hutchcraft's Motel, we watched him load three lard cans full of dressed ducks into a Missouri station wagon one evening.

The next morning we approached him about picking up a

hundred or so ducks for a dinner. I told him that I attracted customers for my tobacco warehouse by throwing wild game dinners and inviting wealthy farmers in.

"By virtue of the fact that I treat them to a good time, plenty of wild meat, booze, and all that stuff, they bring their tobacco to me to sell." He seemed to go for this story. I told him that I'd been able to make considerable money in this way.

Well, he sold us a hundred dressed mallards for $1.75 apiece. I paid him for the birds and we loaded them in the trunk of the new Mercury that the dealer up at Springfield loaned us. (When you are only making about $250 a month as I was then, it's difficult to pose as a wealthy anything.) Bill Summers, the Springfield dealer, was behind us all the way. He saw to it that we were kept in enough new cars to make us look like a bunch of damned millionaires.

We took the mallards that were supposed to have been bought for this tobacco farmers' party back to Nashville and took them out of the lard cans. They were all dressed and frozen, all right, but he'd slipped about ten teal in on the bottom of one of the piles of wild duck.

I immediately called him and raised all kinds of hell. I said, "Look, I paid good money for those birds. I bought mallards and you slipped in a bunch of damned teal on me. They are of no value to me whatsoever!"

Well, he apologized all over himself. "When you come on down here the next time, I'll make an adjustment." We figured we had this fellow in pretty good shape. We made an effort to determine just how extensive his operation was and we found he was supplying black-market ducks to buyers from several states. It was a hell of a big operation.

But we made no effort to close in. Not yet! It was apparent to us that the black-market problem by the end of the season in 1953 in west Tennessee was very serious and that if some drastic action wasn't taken, the ducks using the Mississippi flyway might be in jeopardy of being seriously depleted.

Our undercover work continued. Now we were drinking booze and really living it up, honky-tonking, dropping in on all the night spots and getting pretty well acquainted with all of the local folks down at Reelfoot Lake. We were doing a lot of hunting and buying a few ducks, but we decided to expand our operation.

We moved up to the northern part of the lake and started an undercover operation up there one or two days a week while still giving the man down at Samburg our regular attention.

We made our initial purchase of illegal waterfowl from Hutchcraft in 1953. This black-market business seemed to begin sometime before the legal season opened and extended three or four weeks past the season's close. For the rest of the year, of course, with the ducks gone back to the North, there was little opportunity for these people to take the birds.

During 1954, we were able to determine that this fellow Hutchcraft was a wholesaler. He had several people on the lake who were bringing him surplus ducks, illegally killed by professional guides. These were also ducks they killed on the days they didn't have a sportsman to take out.

That same year, we were able to intensify our efforts in the entire area of west Tennessee and we put in several teams of undercover agents. They always worked in pairs because of the danger of this operation.

We worked on every professional guide in west Tennessee that we could locate. The results were astonishing. There was, we discovered, a large and active market, a loose-knit organization that made a considerable amount of money, up in the tens of thousands, by selling this valuable wildlife resource, the wild duck.

All through 1954, our undercover work proceeded well and we made several valuable contacts. We kept buying more and more ducks from an ever-increasing ring of people and our investigation took on mammoth proportions.

As the season of 1955 approached, we held another meeting in Nashville with Fred Williams and Boots Hammonds. We decided to further intensify our efforts during 1955 because of the five-year federal statute of limitations.

We'd probably break the cases, apprehend, and prosecute these people shortly after the 1955–56 waterfowl season ended.

In the latter part of the season John Drennan had an attack of appendicitis and had to be pulled off the assignment. In his place, I was given a young fellow by the name of Kenneth Stockdale as my partner in this undercover work, which had picked up tempo by now. Ken was new to the business of being a wildlife officer, and was eager and ready to make a "killing." He is now law enforcement chief for the Tennessee Game and Fish Department.

We had an assignment. We were to go to Kenton, Tennessee, a small country town, a few miles southeast of Reelfoot Lake and near the home of the famous Davey Crockett.

We had the name of a man down there, Ted Gaff, and although neither of us had ever seen him, we did have an excellent background on him. We knew exactly where he lived and who he worked for. We knew that he had once worked over a period of years for the Tennessee Gas Transmission Company when they put a major pipeline through the area.

The information that we had received came very late in the season and we had just a few days left. He was thought to be a major supplier of illegal ducks.

So we went over to this little old Tennessee town of Kenton and checked into an old hotel. We could see this man's house from the hotel and were able to watch him when he came home from work. We had an opportunity to get a good look at him. He was a typical, heavyset type. I'd seen lots of these fellows working on pipelines. They are rough, a little too heavy, wear soiled clothes religiously, and all seem to fit into the same mold.

We gave him time to settle down and then we went on over and called to him by name, "Hey, Ted? How've you been, fellow?" We gave him a bunch of that "Hail fellow, well met" stuff, slapped him on the back and all that jazz.

I said, "I don't believe you remember me."

"Well, you know, boy, I really don't believe I do!"

"Well," I said, "my name's Bill Jackson. Don't you recall? We worked on the pipeline together. We used to do a lot of hunting around here."

"Well!" he exclaimed. "I'll be damned, boy! You've put on a little weight."

"Yea, I sure have, but you look good. You look really good!"

"Yea," he agreed. "Everything's lookin' good for me. Come on in and have a drink."

So Ken and I went on in this man's house and sat down and had a drink with him. I told him that I was in the tobacco business, that I'd left the pipeline and had made enough money to buy a tobacco warehouse.

"I'm doing real good," I told him. "But," I said, "I have a big game dinner scheduled for about five weeks away; have all of the farmers up there in Warren and Simpson counties, Kentucky, coming in and I need four or five hundred ducks."

"Well," he said, "I don't have that many, but I do have some and I know people that do have them. I'll take you around and introduce you to them."

So he took us around through the whole damned community and introduced us as old friends that he'd known ever since the pipeline days. These people would sell us without question. We were doing pretty good, but the river bottoms had been frozen over and the opportunity to kill ducks had been seriously curtailed. The market hunters didn't have a great many ducks stockpiled, but we were still buying what we could.

Right in the middle of all of this, on about the third afternoon we were at Kenton, this same man called me at the hotel. "I've found you some birds."

"OK, we'll be right over."

When Ken and I arrived at his house, he told us, "They're over on the other side of town."

"Well, let's go over and have a look at them."

We finally pulled up near a house way out to the edge of this little country town. It was pathetic. A dilapidated rural shack, just a shack with weather-beaten board siding and a rusty tin roof that had come loose from the rafters in places. We had to cross a canal by walking a foot log to get there and this was in January. It was bitter cold.

We went into this house. They still used kerosene lamps and the stink of kerosene was everywhere. There was this frail, shriveled-up woman and four little kids in there. And there wasn't enough furniture to talk about. An old kitchen table and some boxes and one chair.

This fellow introduced us to the woman. "Mrs. Ellsworth, these here men want to buy some ducks."

"Well," she mumbled, "I have four."

It was one of the most pathetic situations I have ever seen in my life. She was preparing some kind of oatmeal gruel or something of that nature for dinner and all of those kids were little and skinny and looked like they were half starved.

Well, she related to me that her husband had been a tenant farmer and that he had been killed in some sort of a tractor accident and that she didn't get any compensation of any sort. She worked only at odd jobs and she really was in desperate straits.

"Where did you get the ducks?" I asked her.

"A man gave them to me."

"Well, why don't you go ahead and cook those birds for your kids? They look like they could enjoy a nice mess of duck."

She shook her head. "If I could get two dollars apiece for them ducks, I could buy a lot more food than I could get outen 'em. We need the money bad!"

"I'll tell you what. I'll give you the eight dollars and you keep the ducks." I made up my mind then and there that this woman was not a market hunter. There was no way she could be a hunter. She looked too frail to pick up a gun, much less shoot a damn duck!

It was just a sad, unusual situation and it was worth the eight dollars of government funds "going out the window" to help her.

There was a nightclub down in this little old town. Obion was a dry county and Kenton lay just inside its border with Gibson County. All Tennessee counties had local option liquor laws and just because we happened to be working in a dry county, this was going to cause us one hell of a lot of trouble later on.

But even if Obion County *was* dry, this nightclub opened wide open. It was a huge concrete block building that also had a restaurant. They served wine with the steak and you could buy whiskey there too.

This is where all of the hunters hung out and, of course, this is where we hung out, too. We spent a great deal of time there during the week or ten days we were working the area in January of 1956.

But we pushed a little too hard.

The last night we were there, we were overly aggressive in trying to buy ducks because we knew that the assignment was closing just as soon as the hunting season closed at the end of the month and we were trying to determine just who was involved and to what extent they were involved.

I believe it was on a Friday night, we had only been able to buy two ducks, which we stored with the rest of the illegal waterfowl that we had been able to collect, in the old hotel where we were staying.

Then about five-thirty, after shooting time, we went down to this nightclub. It was bitter cold that night. Everything was froze over and most of the birds had already gone to open water on the Mississippi River. Almost any possibility of killing any more birds in this section of the state was out of the question.

We had bought a pint of whiskey at the bar and had it setting on the table while we were having dinner. There must have been fifty or sixty people in the place at the time. Outside, it looked just like an old concrete building, but inside it was red hot; it was one of those old-fashioned speakeasy type of places.

While Ken and I were sitting there eating our steak and nipping on the bottle once in a while, suddenly the sheriff and his deputy came in. Stockdale was sitting closest to the door and he saw them first. When he saw that badge, he hid the pint of whiskey down in the breadbasket.

The deputy came over to our table.

"Where are you fellows from?"

"From Bowling Green, Kentucky," I told him.

"What are you doing here?"

"Well, we're just trying to do a little hunting, sheriff."

"Are you trying to buy some ducks?"

I said, "This may be some bad news!"

"No," answered the deputy, "it's all right."

"Well, we picked up a few."

He asked what kind of business we were in and I told him, "The tobacco business."

We talked for a few more minutes and he seemed to be satisfied. He started to leave and then he came back. "You have a hunting license, don't you?"

"Yeah, do you want to see it?"

"I might as well," he replied, so I showed him the license, made out to a fictitious name, William Jackson, with a fictitious address. He studied that for a while and I got out a driver's license made out to the same name to back up what he was reading on the hunting license.

"What's the problem, sheriff? Do we have a problem?"

"No, no problem whatsoever."

Well, the deputy and the sheriff went on to the back of this place where there was this fellow who was drunk and lying on the table. They picked him up and took him out.

This made me a little apprehensive. We were just finishing our steak when this same fellow staggered back into the place and went over to the bar. He kept watching us. I kept noting him.

There was this circular bar around one end of the building and, by now, the place was getting crowded. There were a lot of men in hip boots and hunting clothes. It looked like every damned duck hunter in the county was there that night.

Whiskey was flowing like water, everything was getting a bit lively when suddenly this fellow left the bar and staggered over to our table and sat down. He stared hard at me and although he appeared to be drunk, his eyes were completely clear and in perfect focus.

Suddenly he said, "You follow me." Then he got up and left. Well, I didn't know what to do. I noticed that he went to the back of the building, so I went there, too.

He went into the men's rest room and I followed him. We were standing side by side, each at a urinal, and he turned. All at once he was cold sober and he said, "Look, I don't know who you are and I don't know what your business here is, but let me give you some advice and I won't tell you this but once. Don't leave here with anyone tonight."

This scared the hell out of me because we were in a very bad position if our cover had been blown. As I said before, we had probably pushed too hard and I knew that we had aroused some suspicions. The sheriff and his deputy coming in and questioning us the way they did made me think that we had a problem, a real bad problem.

This fellow in the men's room disappeared and after waiting a minute or so, I went back to our table and sat down. Ken Stockdale and I were sitting there having a drink and I told him in a low monotone, "You go out to the car. Load both shotguns and put them on the back seat." I had a snub-nosed thirty-eight revolver taped up under the front seat on the passenger side.

Well, we really didn't know what to do and so we decided to play it by ear. Ken hadn't much more than got back and sat down at the table when another fellow, dressed in hip boots and canvas hunting coat, came over.

"I understand that you fellows are looking for some ducks."

I answered, "Well, uh, we've got about all we want. How many have you got?"

"I've got seventy-five."

"What do you want for them?"

"Five dollars apiece."

I said, "Hell, that's absolutely ridiculous!"

Then he asked me how much I had been paying for ducks.

"Well, the most I've paid is two dollars. I would pay a dollar and a half for yours, but I don't really want them that bad. I will take them for that though. Maybe I can get some benefit from them."

"Well," he said, "I've got these seventy-five and I will be glad to sell them to you, but I've got to have five dollars apiece."

I shook my head. "No, I don't want them at that price."

He said, "OK," and he went back and sat down at the bar.

Well, there were six or seven fellows around him and they began to do a little talking. Several of them looked our way from time to time.

Our apprehension began to build and Ken and I started to devise ways of leaving the place gracefully. Just about the time we were getting ready to go, this fellow came over and sat down at our table again.

"Look, why don't you wait ten or twenty minutes and I will see if I can pick up another hundred or so birds and you can pick them all up at one time. We'll take less than five dollars for them, but just hang around for a few minutes until I contact some of my buddies and then I will send somebody back in here for you."

"OK," I said, "but we have to go back to the hotel. We want to get in early tonight because the bottoms are all froze up and we will probably get on back late tomorrow afternoon."

So Ken and I sat at the table and continued sipping on this drink we had fixed and some twenty or twenty-five minutes later, this fellow, in a hunting coat and a couple days of whiskers on his face, came in, went to the bar, and ordered a drink. He looked like a lot of these market hunters we had been dealing with. Rough in manner and rougher in clothes. He was a little on the stocky side.

He finished his drink and then came over and sat down at our table.

"Boys, I got one hundred seventy-five birds, all dressed."

I shrugged, feigning not to give much of a damn. "OK, how much?"

"What's your best offer?"

"One-fifty."

"No, I'll have to have two dollars for them."

I shook my head. "No, that's a little more than I can pay. One-fifty is my top offer. Take it or leave it."

"Well," he said, "I'm going to take it."

"OK, where are the birds?"

"My brother has gone out to get the birds. They are out on number seven levee."

"Where in the hell is that?" I asked.

"It's about six miles out of town."

I knew that there was a levee that crossed South Fork river bottom and I also knew that there wasn't a thing on that levee, not a solitary damned thing.

I said, "OK, do you want to take us out there?"

"Yeah, I'll take you out there."

"OK, that's fine. It's a good deal. Are you ready to go?"

The character, dressed in bib overalls under his canvas coat, had on the usual hip boots and slouch hat. It was the uniform of these market hunters.

He got up, so we paid our bill and followed him out of that dive.

We went to Ken's car and put this fellow in the middle. Ken and I had already made our plans. We drove to the middle of this little town of Kenton, then swung right to the hotel.

"Hey! Wait a minute, you should've turned left here."

"No," I answered. "We're going to the hotel for just a minute."

"OK," he said.

So we drove up to the hotel and I said, "OK, Ken, go on in and take care of things."

When Ken left the car, this fellow said, "Wait a minute, what the hell is going on here?"

"Nothing is going on. He'll be back in a few minutes."

The fellow was getting a little nervous. "I've got to make a telephone call."

"Unuh, you are not going to make a telephone call, not now." I slipped that snub-nosed revolver from under the seat of that car and told him, "Just sit tight. Don't move until he gets back."

"I've got to call somebody!"

"Hell no, you're not going to call anybody. Just sit there. Nobody is going to harm you. Just sit still."

He saw the gun for the first time. "My God, that's a pistol!"

"That's right," I said. "And I know how to use it. So you just sit right where you are."

In the meantime, Ken had gone inside, checked us out, got our ducks out of the deep freeze, and got us all set to leave town.

When he came out, he stored all of this stuff in the trunk and back seat. He got in the car behind the wheel.

"Where to?"

"Out of town. Head toward Memphis," I replied.

So we got out of town and about four miles out, I said, "OK, what if we leave you right here?"

We put the guy out beside the road. I don't know to this day the man's name. I don't know to this day what he had to sell, if anything. But I do know damn well that we'd run into a hell of a lot more than 175 ducks if we had gone out to that lonely number seven levee with him. The chances were very good that we wouldn't have come back.

We abruptly terminated this assignment, right there in the middle of the night. We drove to Reelfoot Lake and met with the rest of the undercover team. They had all assembled there at a lodge that the state Game and Fish Commission owned and we matched notes.

Boots Hammonds was actually in charge of the entire investigation. He determined that the investigation in its entirety had been very successful and that now was the time to move in on the market hunters.

Some four or five days later, there was one hell of a roundup of these illegal hunters in west Tennessee. We got several United States marshals and several federal agents from other law enforcement groups and we obtained warrants for all of the people that we had bought migratory waterfowl from.

There were some twenty-six or twenty-eight people involved in this market-hunting activity. It was a crime ring of a sort, dealing in illegal waterfowl exclusively.

We felt that it was very important that we contact all of these people as near to the same time as we possibly could because some of the charges were very serious and some of these "night hunters" might have an inclination to leave the country.

The United States marshals from the Western District of Tennessee and a bunch of Tennessee wildlife officers did the actual serving of the warrants. The five of us who had served as undercover agents, who were the key witnesses in all of the cases, did not participate in the actual arrests. All were brought to Jackson, Tennessee, for arraignment. The warrants ranged from selling migratory waterfowl to possessing over the limit, transporting illegally taken migratory waterfowl, and taking by illegal methods.

We had been watching these people for a period of over two

years. Everyone of them was hit within an hour of the same time. It was real teamwork. There was no resistance. Resistance is relatively uncommon in situations like this. The federal influence is extremely powerful, especially when you are dealing with the hunting element. The minute these market hunters realized that federal authorities had papers for them, they immediately gave in. We have had astonishingly little trouble in the last twenty years in serving arrest warrants on people who had been indicted for similar charges.

These raids gave us a lot of publicity. We had a lot of local people around the western area of Tennessee in bad trouble.

chapter 7

Cajun Country

WHEN I FIRST went to Louisiana as a federal wildlife officer, I was assigned to Breaubridge in St. Martin's Parish. Most of the people in this area speak French.

I was to work with a Louisiana wildlife officer there for a while to, as they put it, be "broken in." This man's name was Noisy Pete Begnaud, a typical Frenchman, dedicated to the task of protecting Louisiana's natural resources. Pete was a small man, about five feet three inches tall and weighing about 130 pounds, but what he lacked in size he made up in enthusiasm for the job. He worked generally as a two-man team and the other half of that team was Easton J. Comier, who usually went by his nickname, Blackie.

When I got in touch with these two men as I was instructed to do, they told me, "Bill, we are going to teach you the basic geography of all of southwestern Louisiana. We're going to teach you about the people down here—their hunting habits and everything that you need to know. And we're going to teach you how to speak some French, because down here in this Cajun country, you're going to need it."

My first patrol with these two fellows was on an August night. We were on a big plantation on the edge of St. Martin's Parish and we caught some night hunters who were shooting rabbits with the aid of a spotlight.

These were very poor people we had caught and they had seven or eight rabbits and the damn rabbits actually stunk. They were gut shooting them and the night was very hot. The rabbits were spoiling about as fast as these night hunters were killing them.

I was astounded by this because never in my life had I heard of a man shooting a rabbit in August, in real hot weather.

These people were Cajuns. They spoke broken English but fluent

French, at least the type of French that was used in that section of Louisiana. I couldn't really understand what was going on that night or what my partners, Begnaud and Comier, were saying to the rabbit hunters. All I knew is that we had to take those damn stinking rabbits along with us as evidence and I was glad when that patrol was over.

Well, these two French-speaking Louisiana state wardens picked me up around seven o'clock and told me that we were going to Iberia Parish where they speak French almost totally because it was apparent to them that I had a lot of it to learn. Speaking French would be helpful.

"I'll be a willing student," I told them, and as we continued on down the road on our patrol that morning, the French lesson got under way.

We'd drive down the damn road and we'd see a duck and they'd say, "*Canard.*" I'd repeat after them, "*Canard.*" That's right, a duck is a *canard.* A mallard is a *canard.*

Then we'd see an old crippled scaup sitting on the canal and Pete would point and say, "*Dogree.*" Yea, a scaup is a *dogree.* All diving ducks are *dogrees.*

"Do you know what a coot is in French?"

"No, I don't."

"Well, a coot is a *poule d'eau.*"

OK, fine! Everything we passed, they gave me the French term for it and I tried to remember it all, repeating it over and over. We were having a great deal of fun and they were being very helpful, but I wasn't well enough acquainted with them to know that they were setting me up for a classic.

"Bill, we are going to teach you a sentence in French. It's about ten words and we want you to memorize this phrase very carefully because we don't want the people down here to know that you are a red-neck. We want them to realize that you, at least, understand our language, and when we get into New Iberia, the parish seat for Iberia Parish, we're going to stop for coffee and we want you to order it."

I said, "That's great, fellows. I really appreciate the trouble you two are taking to teach me French." All the way down the road, I kept practicing this damn phrase, "Voulez-vous coucher avec moi?" I must have kept practicing for the next thirty or forty miles and my tutors would tell me to put a little more emphasis on "coucher avec moi," which I learned to do.

All of this should have aroused my suspicions, but everything was new to me and these two wardens were new to me and I thought, "How nice of them to go to all of this trouble to teach me French!"

Well, we pulled into New Iberia and it was quite a large town, built around the oil industry down there.

We went to a hell of a nice café. We walked in and it was loaded with people. It was about nine o'clock in the morning and that meant coffee time in that section.

My two companions chose a table right in the exact middle of that restaurant and pretty soon, here came a very attractive young lady in a waitress uniform and she came over to our table with pen poised on pad and she said something in French.

I assumed that what she said was something to the effect, "What would you like?" or "What can I get you?"

I let her have this phrase that I had so carefully memorized. "Voulez-vous coucher avec moi?" I said it fast. I knew I had to spill it out before I forgot some of it.

I saw her face go flaming red and she swung at me and I knocked that damned chair over backward as I fell ass over tin cup and I'm telling you those two French game wardens literally got down on the floor and rolled. That was the maddest woman I have ever seen in my life and until you've seen a mad French woman, you just haven't seen anything.

I knew that I must have said something very bad. Well, the entire restaurant was in an uproar. I've never seen a crowd of people laugh as much as those people did. This Noisy Pete Begnaud didn't help quiet things down when he stood up and, in French, explained the whole thing to the whole damned crowd. I've never been so embarrassed in my life and I had to sit there and drink my coffee and act like a good sport while that crowd of people was giving me the big eye the whole damned time I was there! I was afraid to ask what the hell it was that I said and I ignored it for the rest of that day.

When I got back to Breaubridge that night, I called our pilot-agent over in Lafayette. "Joe, if I said this, and you listen carefully, what the hell does it mean?"

He said, "Man, where the hell did you learn that? Don't ever say that to my wife!"

What I did was set there in public with my "bare ass" hanging out and publicly proposition that ol' gal and it damn near got me killed.

Turning that chair over backward was the climax. I saw Pete Begnaud about seven years ago and do you know what the first thing he said was?

"Hey! I never forget the day you made that speech at New Iberia. That ol' gal still asks for you when I go down there. 'Say where that man at, where that red-neck what came down here and told me those things?' "

"Pete, damn you, I ought to kill you for that!"

Those people were loyal, intelligent, hard-working, but they played a lot too and had a sharp sense of humor. Their conversations over the radio were fascinating. They were always in one bad situation after another.

The western Louisiana swamps are divided by the huge Atachalaya Basin and the Louisiana state line. It's a section about 150 miles across and in most areas, the swamp, with its big cypress trees and shadows, is so vast it seems endless.

However, there are some raised areas near the coast and especially in Cameron Parish that have small villages on them. This section is agricultural with rice being the major crop, but the great swamp is as important as the farmland that lies to the north.

The swamps are now, as they were fifty or more years ago, important fur producers and the muskrat here is king. Vast areas of Louisiana swampland were long ago bought up by holding companies simply for the production of muskrat.

Trapping here has always been a highly lucrative business for the natives but, with the importation of the South American nutria, a larger fur-bearing animal that seems to drive the muskrat out and destroys its habitat, the swamps of Louisiana are not what they used to be.

But still sprinkled through these Louisiana swamps are people who live on either houseboats or shacks built up on stilts to escape the high water. These people spend their entire life on the Louisiana swamps. They are people extremely limited in formal education, but are gifted in many respects, including a fine instinct for nature and how to survive in this environment.

They are people whom I learned to admire very much because of their independence and resourcefulness. They use everything they take from the swamp and sell what they don't need. They are descendants of the French Arcadians that came out of Canada a long, long time ago. They seem to be the happiest, easy-come-easy-go sort of people I have ever seen and they are all masters at the arts of fishing, hunting, and trapping. They have little regard for the laws of man. If it's on this earth, they will catch it and either sell it or eat it.

A pirogue or dugout canoe has always been the standard conveyance of these trappers and this unwieldy boat is also an important tool for the game wardens who work these bayous. The first time I got in one, I turned it over five times in less than five minutes and soon became convinced that there was no way a man who wasn't born to these swamps and marshes could ride one of these pirogues. There was just no way it could be mastered by an outsider.

Then suddenly, after playing around with that damned hollowed-out log for the best part of a day, it came to me. The deadly thing about a pirogue is that it is completely soundless and it is highly mobile. They'll run in four inches of water.

In Louisiana, you are dealing with a pirogue tranou, a little ditch through the marsh. Unless you know where they are hidden in the brush and thick marsh grass, you can't "hit" them. That's why, in that entire section of Louisiana, when you are chasing a man in a pirogue, it's really not a hell-for-leather race. You're moving about four or five miles an hour, but so is he. You are both on an equal footing in this one respect. You've got a pirogue. He's got a pirogue.

But there's one exception: That Cajun you're after was born with a push pole in his hands. When you are chasing this man of the swamps and marshes, he'd suddenly disappear. He'd be going down a canal and then simply drop from sight as if the earth had swallowed him, and some of that "back country" looks as if it could, with ageless festoons of Spanish moss hanging from the cypress trees, with the tall grasses and shrubs of the country covering everything.

And you'd search for hours. "Where in the hell did he go?" He just dipped into a pirogue tranou that is overhung with marsh grass. He gets inside, it's almost like a tunnel. He just stays real still and you look and look and look and you never find him unless you know the country and the tricks of these people.

But the one important lesson that I learned down there in bayou country was this: Any show of weakness would get you nothing but grief, and I mean grief! These people are friendly people and what they really expect is simply to be treated with respect and they absolutely insist on the truth.

If a wildlife officer inadvertently misrepresents something to a "Coonass," he won't let the sun set until he's gone back down there and told that Coonass, "I told you this, but after I got back, I found out that I was wrong." And that's acceptable. But if you tell him a lie or misrepresent anything to him either deliberately or inadvertently, then he is finished with you. I don't know where the expression "Coonass" originated, but apparently it is not distasteful to these people of the swamps. They frequently refer to themselves as a Coonass. (And it's quite an acceptable term down there in that section of Louisiana; I've even heard it used in church! It means anybody with a French-Arcadian ancestry.)

Now some of those people who live back in those Louisiana swamps are clean. Their houses are clean and well kept, their person is clean, but there are others back there who live like damn animals. Their houses are filthy and they themselves are filthy.

They might have a nutria-skinning operation going on in the main room of their shack and nutria skinning is very messy because of the great amount of fat that these animals carry. (A nutria is best described as being of the same appearance as a fifteen-pound rat.)

These backwoods people may have anything going on when you pay them a visit, but the crowning insult to a Coonass is if he offers you the hospitality of his home, and you refuse it. He expects you to accept whatever he offers. By virtue of this, I've drunk coffee in places and I've eaten in places that would make the average person deathly ill just to be in the surroundings.

I've had a man who has been skinning nutria all day, with blood and fat up to his elbows on both arms, knock off long enough to make us a pot of coffee without ever washing his hands and that means that there would be a skim of nutria grease on top of that damn coffee cup that was so thick it would hide the coffee under it. I think that's why they make their coffee so damned strong! Otherwise, you couldn't stomach it. It's so strong that you can't taste the nutria grease and if you sort of close your eyes, you can't see it, and if you hold your breath for a second, chances are you won't smell it. But you have to drink that damned coffee as if you are really enjoying it!

But these Cajuns live and enjoy every single solitary day to its fullest. I cultivated them because I enjoyed hearing them tell how life was back in the swamp and I especially related to the older ones who could remember fifty or sixty years ago.

They told how they would make great strikes of muskrat, mostly because the animals were then so plentiful, but also because of the skill of these trappers. They were so wise in the way of the wild that the muskrat didn't have a prayer. They'd catch 'em all. They usually trapped on a sharecrop basis with the owner of the land and they would have such astonishing success that it was not unusual for a trapper to make from twelve or sixteen thousand dollars during a ninety-day season, and that's a pretty damn good income.

But the money came so easy to them that once they became exposed to the outside world, it often went just as easily. One elderly lady, Madame Jim, lived with her husband in the swamp south of Sulphur, Louisiana. She told me about how she and her husband went to Beaumont, Texas, to sell their furs and the total proceeds for their work for that winter was a little bit shy of fifteen thousand dollars.

They had one child. A beautiful little girl about ten years old and she, too, was involved in the entire trapping business, everything from catching the 'rats to skinning them and stretching the hides.

Well, Jim carried his family over to Beaumont and put the girl and woman in a motel. He went on downtown to sell his furs and he demanded the payment in cash.

He was later found in a back alley of Beaumont the next morning, dead drunk and beaten up and without one damned cent. The entire year's work was gone. Jim had taken that huge roll of money and gone into a Beaumont night spot and that took care of that.

But his wife was philosophical about the whole thing. When I asked her, "Didn't you want to kill him?" she shook her head. "Yeah, he made me mad, but then I think, 'Poor Jim, he work so hard so long for that money and he's hurt so bad from losing that money, we just get together and go back to the swamp and make some more money next time.'"

Louisiana has always been a state where violence is second nature. Our efforts in law enforcement and the protection of wildlife met with opposition many times, sometimes serious resistance.

In all cases, the amount and degree of resistance depends upon the temperament of the people you are dealing with. The Louisiana Cajuns, the French Arcadians, are an emotional people. If they are convinced that they are right and you are wrong, they are going to take you on in one fashion or another.

My first exposure to this explosive element in these people came soon after my arrival in Louisiana when I went from my station at Alexandria to Breaubridge during the latter part of August.

They had just begun to harvest rice in this area and while I was driving down a state highway just outside of a town called Rayne, I saw a rice-harvesting operation in a huge roadside field. It was probably at least seventy-five or eighty acres in one spread just off the east side of the highway.

I was driving slow and looking at this because the combines were immense things and there were about nine of them working this huge field. There must have been twenty-five or thirty pickup trucks and larger trucks that were hauling the rice away. There was quite a crew working. It was a big commercial harvesting operation.

Well, lo and behold, as I was driving along, I heard a shot coming from the field. I stopped the damned car and got out to check. I looked and there, on the lead combine, sat a man with a shotgun. I thought, "Well! What in the hell is he shooting?"

Just then, some fifty or sixty feet in front of him, a bird got up and I was able to determine that it was a gallinule and down it came. I heard the shot again.

Well, hell, rice fields are muddy by nature and I wasn't wearing work clothes. I had on slacks, a sports shirt, and low quarter sneakers. I don't have a gun. I don't have a damn thing except a pencil and a badge.

But I have seen the commission of a violation of a federal game law, so I hike my tail out across that damn rice field and finally I get alongside this monstrous combine and start yelling at the operator.

"Hey! Stop that damned machine!"

Well, he wouldn't stop the damned machine and I'm having a tough job trying to keep up, jogging through all that heavy mud.

By this time, the old boy riding shotgun had got alarmed, so he hid the gun down in the rice bin. When I saw that they weren't going to stop the machine, I ran around in front of the combine and forced the driver to either stop or run over me.

This thing had a couple of engines on it and it made one hell of a noise. I tried to tell the driver to get down off the machine, but I never could make him understand. So, I climbed up the ladder that hung down from the cab.

Well, there's the Coonass. There he was and I found three gallinule on top of this combine as well as the shotgun that he had stuck down in the rice. I like to never found that!

So I got the shooter, the gun, and the birds and we came on down off that combine and headed toward my car. We got about halfway across the field and I looked up and noticed about fifty men standing around the damned patrol car.

Some of them were sitting on the hood, others leaning against the sides and back of my car, and all of them sons of bitches had on Levi's, were thin-waisted and barrel-chested, big arms and shoulders and they all looked tough as hell. Everyone of them Coonasses wore cowboy boots and hats.

"Well," I thought, "this is one hell of an introduction to Louisiana!"

The closer I got to that car, the more apprehensive I became. "If anything erupts here, I am a stranger in a strange land." There was no recourse but to go on ahead. I've got this gentleman in tow, along with his gun and his three birds and I walked up to that car just as if I were walking into my yard with a host of my friends waiting for me there.

I opened the door of the car and looked at the ones sitting on the hood. "Get off the car, please."

They got off the car. I put this shooter in the car, got in the driver's seat, and started taking the information from him. "What's your name? Address? Age?"

One of these big fellows, he looked like he might have been the foreman of the crew, stepped up.

"Hey, boy! What are you doing?"

I gave him one of my toughest, most professional stares. "In the first place I am not a boy, and unless you have an official connection with this operation, what I'm doing is none of your concern."

"Hey! Ya say! Like that, huh?"

"Yes, like that." I turned around and resumed my writing. It was difficult to keep my right hand from shaking because I could sense things weren't good and I was afraid that this loud-mouthed son of a bitch, who asked what I was doing, was going to blow the whole thing up.

Once trouble started with this bunch, I knew that there'd be a physical encounter with the mood they were in. Well, it would be just "too wet to plow."

"Well," the leader said, "this man works for me."

"Then if this man works for you, if he is an employee of yours, I think that you are entitled to know what I am doing here. I am a federal law enforcement agent and I have taken this man into custody for killing gallinule from a motor-driven vehicle and, besides that, the season isn't open either."

"Oh," he said, "I see, you're a game warden."

"That's what I am."

"Oh, that's fine, that's fine. We'll just pay that fine."

I replied, "Well, the amount of the fine is not set by me. I have nothing to do with the fine. I am going to take the information from him. If you fellows behave yourselves, I'm going to give him a summons and leave him here with you."

Hell, it was my first day in the state and I had no idea where to take him if I had wanted to!

Well, I'll be damned if they didn't just stand there, watching. They said a lot of degrading remarks, light remarks with a touch of humor, but most of it was in French and I couldn't understand what it was they were really talking about. I did pick up "Le Game Warden" and then they'd all laugh like hell. I didn't know whether they were saying, "You take him on this side," or "I'll take him on the other," or what the hell they were saying, but I had put into practice a lesson I learned early in this business. If you face up to a lawbreaker or even a whole damn crowd and give the appearance of not being frightened, most of the time you can deal with them and come out of it with your skin in one piece.

During this tour of duty in Louisiana, I was also exposed to the seemingly endless marsh and swamps to the southwest and southern part of the state. This wild country begins at the Gulf and protrudes inland for as much as a hundred miles in some places. This marshland extends up the Mississippi River on both sides as well as around the Atachalaya Basin, an old Mississippi River cutoff that is probably centuries old. This is a marsh and a swamp with huge old cypress trees combined and I don't think that there is anything like it anywhere else in the country.

It has always been a land teeming with wildlife, and the outlook of these people who have lived here for centuries is beautiful. Their basic philosophy is simply "All of this bounty was placed here by the Lord for my taking as I see fit." The people of the Louisiana wetlands are very religious. They live close to God's great earth.

"If the Good Lord didn't want them teal shot in August, He wouldn't have sent them down here in August. If He wanted us to wait until November to shoot ducks, He wouldn't have the ducks here until November. If He didn't want us to shoot teal when the great spring migrations are headed north, He'd have sent them out of here in late January rather than have them stay through February, March, and April."

This philosophy was beautiful in a sense, but it was ultradestructive. These were the days when the deep-freeze units were coming onto the market and along with the swell of population in the coastal states, a huge black market for wild game was created.

I spent endless nights on those bayous and marshes of Louisiana. The country was unbelievably beautiful and mysterious at night, except for the mosquitoes! Down there they came in the giant size and in hordes. Those damned mosquitoes seemed to be starved and they would eat a man alive!

It was during this time, in the middle fifties, that the American alligator was plentiful in this area, particularly in the wildlife refuges. There were some huge 'gators there and as a result there was also quite a lot of poaching. It was my responsibility, of course, to eliminate this.

I was on the Lacassine National Wildlife Refuge, down below Lake Arthur one night, working alone down a canal and paddling my boat so as to make as little noise as possible, when I heard a shot. It was somewhere around eleven o'clock at night.

I eased the boat on down the canal for another three quarters of a mile and pulled up on a spoil bank where the dredgings from the canal had been dumped. With the aid of binoculars, I could see a man out in a pool inside the refuge trying to move a huge alligator from the pool over to the levee where he had left his boat.

I tied up my own boat and walked on down to where I was about twenty or thirty feet from the poacher and then waited until he got the alligator (it was about an eleven footer) on top of a spoil bank. From there, he had a downhill drag to get the 'gator in his boat.

Then I turned the light on him. I recognized Peg Leg Herbert, a notorious alligator poacher from around Lake Charles. He didn't offer any resistance and I took his gun. He used an old Model 97 Winchester and he was shooting these aligators with the shotgun loaded with a single slug or a punkin' ball. This combination does a deadly job on even the largest of alligators. You've got to kill them dead at the first shot or, generally, you'll lose them.

Well, anyhow, I had this man out there miles from nowhere in the dead of night. After I had taken the necessary information from him, I had him help load this huge alligator into my own boat (which must have really added insult to injury as far as he was concerned).

My boat was just fourteen feet long and with the alligator measuring eleven foot, there wasn't a hell of a lot of room left. The only way we could get that dead alligator into that damned boat was to put his nose down and work it up into the bow and under the cockpit cover. I left about four and a half feet of his tail sticking outside the cockpit and I had to sit on that tail in order to operate the boat.

Well, I unloaded the old bird's gun, gave it back to him, and told him that he would be notified when to appear in court. Then I sent him on his way because I had heard another shot on the other side of the refuge.

I cranked up the motor on my boat and started on down this canal. The night was so peaceful and quiet and I was running real slow with the engines muted.

Everything was lovely. I was getting into position to nail another poacher when this dead alligator, whose tail I was using for a seat, gave a convulsive jerk, whacking me under the arm with the tip of that long tail, and damned near knocked me out of that boat!

I almost left that eleven-foot alligator, with a fourteen-foot Lone Star runabout, with a forty-horsepower motor on it, all to himself. I doubt very seriously if he could ever have driven it, but that 'gator almost got the chance.

After that hassle, I went around to the other side of the refuge and I caught two fellows over there with three small alligators, from about two and a half to four feet long.

Well, I loaded those 'gators on top of the big one and went back to refuge headquarters, getting there about three o'clock in the morning. I tried to load that big 'gator in the trunk of my car because I wanted my kids to see it. It must have weighed five or six hundred pounds but, of course, it just wouldn't fit. I would get one end of the critter in the trunk in some fashion, then when I was shoving on the other end, the first would fall out.

I never did make it. The refuge boys helped me skin that alligator the next morning and skinning a monster that tough and large is one hell of a job. That skin—the largest I'd ever seen—was worth saving for display at the refuge headquarters.

Those Louisiana Cajuns knew all of the shortcuts. They could cook anything—crawfish, crabs—anything wild, and they knew how to make it a real delicacy.

I've never seen a wild duck that I could enjoy eating. One Thanksgiving, we were invited over to Louis LeLeau's house for dinner. (Louis was a Louisiana state conservation officer with whom I worked.) When we got there, I was dismayed to note that his wife, Belle, had duck—duck with oyster dressing and rice.

Well, we sat down with this family and knowing the Cajun feeling about their guests accepting whatever was offered, I figured that I would, at least, try a little bit of that duck and a little bit of that dressing just to be polite, and because that was what was expected of me.

Well, to make a long story short, those full-grown pintails didn't last long and that dressing, I can still taste it. It was the best I've ever had. Belle LeLeau was probably the best damned cook in Louisiana and there are a lot of them down there. We enjoyed being with these people. I worked with Louis LeLeau for the entire year I was down there in Louisiana.

Small boys (top) *are Willie Parker* (right) *and brother Richard.* PHOTO COURTESY OF WILLIE J. PARKER. Above: *Willie Parker in his early days as a Tennessee Game Warden.* PHOTO BY WALLACE DANLEY, TENN. CONS. DEPT.

Above: *Slim Durbin, who at first was antagonistic toward Parker and later changed his attitude.* PHOTO BY RONNIE PARKER, COURTESY OF WILLIE J. PARKER. Below: *Pat, the black Labrador retriever that was a "Federal agent," pauses with Parker during duck survey.* PHOTO COURTESY OF WILLIE J. PARKER.

On waterfowl nesting grounds in Canada, Parker uses special pliers to crimp identification band onto leg of redhead duck without injuring bird (note additional bands on big ring around Parker's neck). Reports of recovered bands are great help in monitoring waterfowl migrations. PHOTO COURTESY OF WILLIE J. PARKER.

Top: *Ducks taken illegally in corn-baited trap would have been sold or eaten by Maryland poachers if Federal agents had not intervened.* PHOTO COURTESY OF WILLIE J. PARKER. Above: *These ducks were confiscated from poachers on Maryland's Eastern Shore. Agents then cut open the crop of each bird for evidence of feeding on illegal corn bait.* PHOTO BY BILL BURTON, BALTIMORE SUNPAPERS.

Above: *Some of the 500,000 geese that spend the winter in Dorchester County on Maryland's Eastern Shore, rise from Blackwater Marsh for flight to nearby cornfields to feed.* PHOTO COURTESY OF WILLIE J. PARKER. Below: *On opening day of goose season, Parker* (third from left with pipe in his mouth) *fills out summonses for hunters found hunting illegally over bait. Facing hunters and camera is a fellow game warden.* PHOTO BY BILL BURTON, BALTIMORE SUNPAPERS.

Closeup shows the lines that have developed in Parker's face since his early days as a game warden. Parker's favorite motto is: "The Good Lord hates a coward." PHOTO BY CONWAY ROBINSON.

Opposite page: *Cindy Delaney* (top) *is equally effective in work on fish and wildlife projects or as an undercover agent.* PHOTO COURTESY OF WILLIE J. PARKER. *Parker himself* (below) *is shown in a typical working environment, paddling his pirogue from one point to the next.* PHOTO BY JIM PHILLIPS.

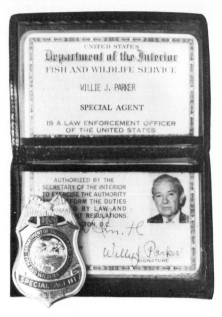

Parker's badge and credentials identify him as Special Agent, U.S. Department of the Interior, Fish and Wildlife Service. PHOTO COURTESY OF WILLIE J. PARKER. Below: In Parker's Nashville, Tennessee, office he talks with co-author Conway Robinson. The office is the nerve center of operations in Tennessee, Kentucky, and North and South Carolina. PHOTO BY GEORGE GREEN.

chapter 8

Night Hunters of Louisiana

ON THE NINETEENTH of August 1957, I reported to Alexandria, Louisiana, for duty, went down to southwestern Louisiana, and went to work.

At the time I think there were only seven federal wildlife agents in all of Louisiana, and this was just about one-third enough. They should have had at least twenty-five officers in that state and they are still seriously understaffed down there.

Afternoon upon afternoon, from just before sundown until well after dark, a solid canopy of pintails and mallards came out of the swamps to feed in the rice fields. It was a beautiful, unforgettable sight!

It was just amazing to stand on a levee and watch these Louisiana waterfowl. I often stayed out there until long after dark and listened to them winging across the bayou country. You could hear their wingtips cross, you could hear them "talk" to each other, hear the whistle of the fast-flying pintails and the chatter of the mallards as they were going to the feeding grounds. Then I would be up at three-thirty or four the next morning to hear the wild ducks return from the rice fields back to the swamps again.

Night hunting was very prevalent down there in the Louisiana bayou country. The people had devised a method. On those moonlit nights when soft white clouds were floating in from the Gulf and when those ducks were feeding in the rice fields, that was the best time to shoot them.

It was fantastic to hear a duck call being used in the still of the night. The call was always muted, always a soft quack, never a long drawn-out call. I'd hear the "Quack, Quack" then "BOOM!" One shot. Unbelievable, effective, hard to locate.

After working on those moonlit nights and in those lonely bayous and marshes, and having those ducks flying within twenty feet of me, it was apparent that the Louisiana night hunters had worked out a deadly method. There was a lot of trouble between the federal agents and the night hunters.

One night I was working south of Lake Charles with two state conservation officers, Lloyd Andrus, who had flu, and Louis Le-Leau, who had an injured back. In fact, he was later operated on for a slipped disk.

We heard shooting in a rice field. We drove in that direction with no lights, complete blackout, and I pulled off the road to just set tight in the car. I decided that I could slip in this way and take this night hunter. There was only one shot at a time and I assumed that it was just one hunter.

This rice field was huge. It was a beautiful night, but it was very windy. I had the wind in my favor because it was blowing from the hunter to me.

I had parked the car almost in the center of the rice field and we were extremely close to the call and the shooting. We could see the fire coming from the gun. That rice field was alive with pintails.

"Stay here in the car," I told the two agents who were incapacitated. I worked my way up to a point about fifty yards from the shooting. I was crawling on a levee, a ridge built up to center irrigation water, and it was damn wet work. This was February. The rice had been harvested in September or October, but the levees remained. There was water between them still.

Suddenly, I saw two figures get out of a sunken blind. These night hunters usually sank fifty-five-gallon drums in the fields and hunted from them.

Well, these two figures came toward me. I could easily see them in the moonlight. At first I thought that they were on the same levee that I was on, but these levees meandered and when these hunters got about twenty-five yards from me, they turned and took an oblique direction away from my position.

Well, the wind was still in my favor. It was quite warm, even in February in these sections of Louisiana. I wore a wool shirt, hunting trousers, and tennis shoes. In these patrols down there, you were often wet and with that type of clothes, especially the wool socks, you could dry yourself out quite rapidly if you had the opportunity. You weren't too uncomfortable too long.

I crossed to their levee when I saw that these two hunters were moving away from me, and then I started running, depending upon the wind to keep any sound from alerting them to my presence.

I finally got some ten yards from them. We were all on the same levee now. I saw them stop and knew that they had heard me.

I turned my flashlight on them. "Federal agents! Drop your guns!"

By this time, I had my pistol in my hand because things happen rather rapidly down in those Louisiana rice fields.

Well, they both fell to the levee.

I took two more steps.

I heard one of them say, "KILL HIM!"

When he said that, I hit the ground. The man fired twice, right over my head. My head at point-blank range! Well, this scared the living hell out of me.

As I recall, I heard one of those guys working the action of a pump gun and for some reason, I turned the light on. We were about twenty feet apart. I had been mistaken by the way the levees twisted and turned. Actually they were on another levee running parallel to the one I was on.

One of these guys was trying to load his gun and the action on the other's gun had jammed and he was trying to clear it.

I fired point-blank at the night hunter who was trying to load his gun. He went off the levee backward and I thought, "Well, my God, this is terrible. I've hurt a man!"

I turned to pull off a shot at the other man but he was up and running. Well, I jumped up, crossed the water between the levees, a distance of twenty-five feet, and gave chase, ran him for a considerable distance. We were evidently running in a sort of large circle. I detected a second figure, joining the first, and he was running with his right hand holding his left side. (Later we determined that there was blood all over that damned levee.)

Well, I was gaining on them. I was pretty fast afoot and once again I got within twenty-five or thirty feet from them and I shouted, "Stop or I'll shoot!"

When I said this, the one who retained his gun, who hadn't been hit, turned and fired directly at me. Fortunately, I hit the ground in time again and from this prone position, I turned on the light and fired at him, five times, slow fire.

Well, he was cutting that rice field to pieces. He was really dancing. He was zigzagging and hell, I didn't even touch him.

Without stopping to think about my gun being empty, and in the heat of the chase and everything, they kept running and I ran too. I was a couple of hundred yards behind them by this time. We came to a wide canal. The two men I was after had already swum this canal and had hid in a field of tall weeds. Well, without thinking, I swam this canal too. I still had my flashlight. The canal was shallow, just a little bit over your head.

I climbed up into the field, turned on my flashlight. I was determined to find those two fellows.

But then, all at once, it came to me! I have an empty pistol in my hand, I have no additional cartridges, and *I'm* looking for two people, one I know has a shotgun and apparently plenty of ammunition and it is apparent to me that he is not one darned bit hesitant to use it.

So, suddenly realizing where I was and what my circumstances were, I turned the light off, walked to the car, and got the two state wildlife officers who had come out in the field to assist me, but we were unable to locate the scene of the trouble.

We picked up nineteen pintails, a hunting coat, four boxes of shells, and a gun. The gun was in the water, where the man I had shot dropped it.

The next evening we canvassed the entire area and alerted the Federal Bureau of Investigation in trying to determine who these two people were. To this day, I don't have the slightest idea who they were, where they were from, or what it was all about, but they did teach me an invaluable lesson: You just don't get careless when you are dealing with people who violate the law. Even though most people in the hunting community are good people, there are some bad ones and some, even, who are very dangerous.

I went back to my station the next morning and that incident stayed with me, on my mind all day.

"Well! It's bad that I'm not as good a pistol shot as I should be, so I will take an M-1 carbine with me on these night patrols from now on."

Well, late the next morning, I went back up there with the same two state conservation officers and we wondered, "Do you think that those fellows could possibly come back?"

We agreed to ease down there and see. About nine-thirty that night we drove down there and parked the patrol car in a position where we could hear shooting coming from this same field.

We hadn't been out of the car three minutes before we heard a BOOM, a single shot coming from the exact location where we'd heard the shooting the night before.

Well, cold chills went up and down my spine! I said, "All right, tonight I'm going to take them!" I got the carbine out of the car, loaded it, put one in the chamber.

The two state agents who were with me were still ill. They weren't able to accompany me, although they did manage to go part of the way.

I got on the same levee that I was on the night before and it was a terrible feeling. The shooting was coming from the precise blind that it had been coming from the night before. It was unbelievable! Unreal! The closer I got, the more apprehensive I became about engaging these people in a situation that I was sure would erupt violently into gunfire the minute I made my presence known.

I don't know what the difference is between a brave man and a coward. Sometimes I don't think that there is very much. Probably the brave man is just too obstinate or too hardheaded to admit that he is really a coward.

Well, I continued on down this levee until I got to about fifty feet from the shooting location and it was a replay of the night before. Two men got up out of the same blind. I could see them well. It was a still night this time, no wind blowing. They had pintail. I could see the white of the pintail drakes. They had the ducks slung over their shoulders and both men carried shotguns. This time they came out on the same levee that I was on.

There is very little cover on a rice field levee but, luckily, there was some vegetation growing on the side of this one at the edge of the water. I took advantage of this vegetation and concealed myself as I slowly worked my way down the levee.

I was confident that it had to be the same two people or, at least, one of the two whom I had encountered the night before.

As they came toward me, that fifty-foot distance seemed like ten miles. When they got up to where I was concealed, I jumped up out of the grass with the safety off that carbine, socked it in the first man's stomach, and turned on the light.

"Drop your guns or I'll kill you!"

Well, this was one hell of a way to introduce yourself. They dropped their guns promptly and up went their hands.

"OK, now back away from your guns."

They did so.

"All right, get some identification out." I had them then. Had 'em in the light, had the carbine up where I could handle it with one hand.

Well, they got some identification out all right and my God! I was astounded! One was a schoolteacher and the other one was a businessman, both from Lake Charles.

And this was closed season, at night, and they had a string of pintail.

After I determined that they didn't present any danger to me and that they were just ordinary people taking a chance by violating the federal game laws and getting caught, I tried to be real nice and erase the memory of this figure coming out of the stillness of the night and poking a carbine, a very lethal weapon, into the belly of a reputable schoolteacher!

They were frightened. Badly frightened.

I seized the ducks, took the information from them, and escorted them to where they had their car hidden, and sent them back to Lake Charles.

The courts, even at that time, were very sensitive about the use of a deadly weapon and I was very anxious about the fact that I had used a carbine on this gentleman coming out in testimony in federal court.

"Well," I thought, "possibly I'll get by. Maybe they'll plead guilty and we'll just give a statement of facts and it won't come out in court that I did pull a carbine on this man!"

Some one or two months later, the case came to trial before Judge Hunter in the United States District Court at Lake Charles.

I was apprehensive as hell.

These two defendants were already there and they weren't too friendly when I came in. Judge Edwin F. Hunter, Jr., called the case. They came up and entered a plea of guilty.

Judge Hunter was a very fine United States district judge and he was very concerned about the rights of an individual. He very carefully explained the defendants' rights to them, but he did accept their plea of guilty.

Prior to sentencing them, he asked, "Do you have anything you want to say in court before sentencing?"

Well, I didn't breathe. I thought, "Man! If I get over this hurdle, I've got it made. Perhaps the carbine business won't come out."

The businessman said, "No, Your Honor, I have nothing to say."

Then the schoolteacher spoke up. "Yes! I'd like to ask a question."

Judge Hunter said, "Go right ahead."

Well, hell, I knew what was coming.

The schoolteacher asked, "I'd like to know what right the agent had to stick a machine gun in my stomach and tell me, if I didn't drop my gun that he was going to kill me."

Well, this scared the living hell out of me because I have always been a little bit awed by the United States courts.

Judge Hunter immediately asked, "Which agent made this case?"

Of course, I had to stand before him and say, "I did, Your Honor."

"Agent Parker, where did this incident occur?"

"It was south of Lake Charles, Your Honor. In fact, it was in the same field I was shot at the night before!"

The judge said, "Oh, I see!"

He turned to the schoolteacher and spoke harshly. "Sir, these agents work alone. They work at night and they work against terrible odds. I suggest that if you don't want to feel the end of their gun muzzles that you stay at home during the closed season, where you belong."

Well, this made me feel like a tiger and very good. I thought that it was a very apt expression uttered by Judge Hunter. He fined each of those two gentlemen five hundred dollars and put them on a year's probation, forbidding them to hunt migratory waterfowl for the term of the probation. I breathed a sigh of relief when that one was over!

I had followed an agent down there by the name of Paul Cole, and Cole was a lone wolf. He worked by himself. Although he refused to work with anyone else, he was a very effective agent. He had a cadre of informers down there in that bayou country that kept him posted as to what was going on. He dealt with the destructive hunting elements efficiently and effectively. He checked very few hunters routinely. He'd go after the night hunters, the waterfowl baiters, the market hunters, and those who shot over limit, and he went after some bad ones in the process.

Many's the time I have stepped out at night and said, "Federal agent, lay your gun down!"

And the man would say, "Are you Paul Cole?" And I could detect the terror in his voice.

"Lay the gun down!"

And after he'd lay the gun down, I'd say, "No, I'm not Paul Cole, but I am a special agent, so leave it down."

There were a lot of market hunters whom Paul Cole had brought to justice and there were a lot of market hunters down there in Louisiana who would have killed Paul Cole if they'd had the chance.

One man down there told me that he and two of his brothers had put the word out that they were going to kill Paul Cole. They had a live decoy pen that was heavily baited and they were waiting for a certain time to shoot it.

They had been drinking and they didn't realize that while they were doing all this talking, one of Cole's informers was sitting right there at the bar alongside of them.

Cole knew precisely when and where they were going to shoot. They were going to shoot about eight o'clock in the morning and they had set up an elaborate guard system in the bayou. They planned to take Paul Cole cold when he came in after them. They figured that he'd be there.

Well, he got there before they did. He was in their blind while they were busy making all those elaborate preparations to trap him when he came in!

Paul knew from the direction of the wind which creep blind they would shoot. They had a blind on either side of this pond deep in the swamp. This was to be a mass shoot of the ducks that had been brought into the area with bait and live decoys.

Well, Paul let them shoot. They had to come over to the blind he was hiding in to pick up the dead birds and when they did, Paul stood up with a carbine. They felt secure because of the guards they had posted. "Paul can't get in here alive!" But the hell of it was, he was already in there with a carbine leveled at the market hunters.

"Stand where you are!"

And they did.

From his actions, they knew that he wasn't afraid of them and from that carbine in his hand, it was apparent that he had come equipped to do any kind of business they chose.

He was able to take them into custody without any problems. In fact, the guards they had posted were very surprised to see him coming out from behind them with their three buddies in tow. There were six of them in all, but he couldn't connect the guards with the operation, so he just rolled out with the hunters and the confiscated ducks. He did take the time on his way out to stop to talk to the guards who were posted to kill him.

Paul Cole developed a reputation down there in southeastern Louisiana that remains to this day. There are people there who will remember Paul Cole and tell one of a thousand stories about him if you ask.

Cole knew these people. They were the type who called for a show of force. But once you made your move, once you got over the initial encounter when you stepped out and identified yourself as a federal wildlife officer, you could relax. It was during this initial encounter when violence would happen if it was going to happen. It could come in many forms.

I was involved in a situation down there where a state wildlife officer probably kept me from getting the living hell beat out of me. I was opposing one of the strongest poachers I had ever seen. I was trying to take his shotgun away from him and I couldn't. I simply couldn't disarm this man, he was too powerful.

Louis LeLeau was with me. I had a few minutes of a very bad time while I was trying to take that gun away from the lawbreaker, because I knew the damn gun was loaded. He had refused to identify himself. He had refused to show his license or duck stamp and he had refused to surrender his gun, so I took him on, but I used very bad judgment in doing so.

During all of this trouble, Louis, who was getting on in age, was sitting in the patrol car waiting for me. When I didn't return in a reasonable time, he got worried and came out to check.

He found this giant Cajun and me tearing up the swamp, so Louis stepped into it and stuck a gun in the man's ribs.

"Drop your gun!"

That gentleman did so, so quickly that I fell ass over teakettle right there in that damn mud. I hadn't even seen Louis come up. He was like a cat even at that age when he should have been retired, and besides, that son of a bitch was requiring all of my attention.

chapter 9

Kentucky Wonders

I WAS TRANSFERRED to Murray, Kentucky, in May of 1958. Murray is a little farming community not far from the long Kentucky Lake. Captain Robert Soaper had retired as agent in charge of Kentucky at the time I came into the area. I was sent there to take over.

Back then, Kentucky Lake was one of the finest fishing spots on earth. I worked the western part of the state for two and a half years. The work was rather routine. There were some waterfowl in this area and we made a few hits and a lot of well—insignificant cases.

Then suddenly, out of the clear blue, they transferred me, in 1960, to Henderson, Kentucky, a farming community of perhaps twenty thousand people. Henderson lay right on the Ohio River in the northern section of the state and just about as close to the border with Indiana as you could get.

Working in this part of Kentucky was one of the most exciting and satisfying experiences of my life. I don't know to this day why I was transferred there, evidently somebody felt that the people in this area were a problem and that I could do something about it.

They let me know that I was to be there in time for the opening of dove season, September 1! This gave me exactly four days to get moving, but things moved fast in those days, including me!

I went to Henderson the next morning with Faye and we rented a house and moved into it, with our two kids, Ronnie and Rita, on the last day of August!

By this time we had acquired a dog, a young Labrador retriever bitch named Pat. Pat was from one of the first and finest bloodlines in this part of the country.

My young son, Ronnie, was frightened of dogs, so I wanted to get a dog he could become used to, especially a hunting dog. I had enjoyed dogs all my life and I felt that my son would be less fearful of them if we had one around the house. So I bought Pat. I got her from a kennel owner, Jimmy Myatt of Barlow, Kentucky. Jim had his own mind when it came to breeding and selling his fine Labradors and I was soon to find this out.

There was this litter of puppies down there in the Myatt kennels, nine of them. Eight were males, beautiful, huge, square-headed—typical field-trail-type Labs. The other, the runt of the litter, was a little female. She was bottle-nosed, had none of the characteristics of the field trail or hunting strain of Labrador.

However, all of the male pups were just lying around the kennel on their backs with their huge paws sticking up in the air. Meanwhile this awkward-looking little bitch pup was stalking butterflies all over that kennel. She was jet black, active, intelligent, but very small.

Well, that ol' boy, Jim Myatt, wanted a hundred dollars apiece for those male pups and that was a little more than I could afford.

"How much will you take for the bitch?"

The kennel owner shook his head. "She ain't fer sale."

"Why?"

"Well, she just didn't breed true. She's bottle-nosed and very small."

So I asked him what he planned to do with her.

"Well, we'll probably put her to sleep."

I told the man, "Look, Myatt, she's just what I want! What *would* you take for her?"

He shook his head. "Nope, won't sell her to you. I couldn't sell her at any price."

Well, after a lot of haggling and persuading on my part, he finally agreed to sell me that little pup for thirty-five dollars, if I agreed to have her spayed prior to the time that she came into her first heat.

So I bought Pat, that ungainly little Labrador pup, under those conditions and she turned out to be one of the delights of my life.

I didn't have much time for Pat with dove season open in Kentucky. I worked both Warren and Simpson counties and caught quite a few baiters and over-the-limit shooters. They got a course in conservation that cost them quite a bit of money. It was a "cram course" before some tough federal judges!

On the second day of September I got back home very late at night and it was hot. I was trying to get an air-conditioner installed in the casement-type window and that is not an easy chore.

I had planned to have that damned air-conditioner installed by the next day at eleven-thirty, which would give me time to take a shower and get myself out in the fields for the shooting hours, which began at twelve noon. Well, things just didn't go right. The damned air-conditioner wouldn't fit and by one o'clock I was still working on it.

But about four hundred yards from my house in Henderson, shooting began abruptly at noon and I could hear the gunfire while I was working on that air-conditioner. The shooting increased in intensity.

"Well," I said to myself, "I had better just go over there and see what this is all about." I was in dungarees, had on a T-shirt and tennis shoes, and was all dirt from head to foot from having been working on that damned air-conditioner.

When I got to the scene of the shooting, I found an old mine entrance and a huge area that was completely cleared of vegetation, nothing but cinders, just cinders.

There were about nine men standing in a huge circle around this area and I wondered, "Well, what in the hell would bring mourning doves into this kind of place?"

I walked up to the first man. "How're you doing?"

He grinned. "We are killing 'em!"

I nodded. "It looks like they are flying pretty good."

"They sure are," he agreed.

"What are they coming in to?"

"We got it loaded!" he replied.

"With what?"

"Cracked corn, man! They're really coming in here! Where's your gun?"

I said that I'd left it at the house, that I had just walked over to see what all the shooting was about.

"Well," he answered, "we're sure having a ball this afternoon!"

Then I told him. "You know, I've got some sad news for you."

"What's that?" he asked.

"I'm a federal game warden. I want you to just keep smiling and get your license out of your pocket and hand it over to me and don't say a damn word to anybody! You stop your shooting, but you just stand there with your gun in your hands and look up at the sky just like you've been doing."

Well, the man got white as a sheet. I took his license, put it in my pocket, walked around to the next man in the circle real slow.

"Hi, how are you doing?"

"Oh," he replied, "we're tearing them up, really tearing them up. I've already got five and it's still early."

"Yes," I agreed, "it certainly is." I also told him I was a federal game warden. "Let's have your license and don't you move. Don't say anything!"

Well, I finally rounded up seven of those guys the same way, got seven licenses. As I took the hunting license from the seventh, the last two dove shooters in the circle noted that things had got awfully quiet. As I came around toward them, they broke and ran.

I was rather fleet of foot at that time of my career, so I had little trouble in running them down, one after the other. When I had finally rounded them all up and checked their credentials, I discovered that one was a local minister and another was a member of the Henderson Police Department!

I left them waiting there in my yard while I went on in the house, took a quick shower, slipped on fresh working clothes (my uniform), got my summons book, and wrote them all up, using the hood of my car as the "desk."

Then I proceeded on with my patrol. That was some afternoon. I'd barely got out to the edge of town when I saw that the car in front of me had two young fellows in it, with a shotgun sticking out of the right window.

I followed them.

Suddenly they stopped. They had seen a dove sitting on a

telephone wire along the road. They promptly bucked him off the wire and down he came.

OK. I stopped them and wrote them up.

Then, by accident, I found myself in Horseshoe Bend, a huge segment of old river bottoms below Henderson. There were very few buildings here and those that were there were shacks built on high poles or stilts to prevent the flood waters from getting into the buildings.

Once this section was rich, beautiful farmland, and there were still a couple of old houses down there and a few corncribs. There was also one hell of a population of mourning doves in the area.

I got down almost to the end of the bend and I noticed two fellows on the side of the road ahead of me. I eased on down, cutting my speed. This was an old country road, dirt, not paved, and as I drew closer, these two characters stepped out into the middle of the road.

Of course, I had to either stop or run them down, so I stopped.

One of them carried a shotgun, but the other fellow was the one who really got my attention. He was at least six feet tall, had on an old black, slouch hat, and was chewing tobacco. It was dribbling out the sides of his mouth.

They just stood there in the middle of that damned road. Well, this tall fellow had on bib overalls and by this time, I could detect that he had what looked like a "smoking" thirty-eight western-style pistol on a belt strapped tight over his overalls.

"This," I thought to myself, "is rather unusual." I stopped directly in front of them, not three feet away. And then I noticed something else. That tall ol' boy had a pint whiskey bottle sticking out of the hip pocket of his overalls. He was, it seemed, rather well prepared for anything.

"Good afternoon," I said.

The tall fellow took a big chew of tobacco and looked me over for a while. "What's good about it?"

"Well," I answered, "that was just supposed to be a sort of a greeting, but if you don't think that there is anything good about it, well then, I don't suppose there is. But will you step aside? I want to go on down in these bottoms."

The tall fellow replied, "I don't think that you are going anywhere. I think that the best thing you can do is just turn that car around and get the hell out of here!"

I believe that this fellow was the meanest-looking man I've ever seen in my life. I thought, "Well! Here we go! We might as well get this matter settled right now, because I'm going to be in these bottoms every day and I don't intend to have this type of altercation every time I come down here."

"Let me introduce myself," I replied. "I'm Bill Parker, and I am a federal game warden and you can do one of two things. You can either get the hell out of my way or you can consider yourself under arrest and get into the back seat of this damned car!"

Then the tall, tough guy really surprised me. "Well, hell, you don't have to get mad."

"I'm not mad. I don't get mad. Just do one of two things. You either step aside or you get in the car."

"Well," he muttered, "we'll step aside."

And they did.

I went down into the lower end of the bottoms and checked a few hunters. When I came back out, there were those same two fellows still there in the same spot beside the road.

They flagged me down. "What do you mean, you're a federal game warden?"

"I enforce the federal game laws." They looked as if they still didn't understand. "I arrest people who violate the game laws, like shooting doves over bait."

"Oh?" This seemed to satisfy them and I had no more trouble that day.

I later found out that the tall ol' boy's name was Slim Durbin. He was an old bachelor who lived down in the bottoms. Later we got to be fast friends.

After that, when I knew that the Ohio River was up and Slim was cut off (he didn't have a boat) and had no way to get into town during high water, why I'd go down to his shanty about twice a week in my own boat to check on him.

I'd take his order for supplies and that order went something like this:

He wanted about four pounds of bacon, he wanted about four pounds of bologna, two dozen eggs and about four loaves of bread. But most important of all was the two cases of beer and four fifths of whiskey!

I guess it was pretty lonesome down in those bottoms when the Ohio River was less than a foot and a half or maybe two feet under your bed!

chapter 10

A Boy and His Goose

DONAN JENKINS, THE state wildlife officer for Kentucky, and I worked up there in the Henderson County area, and he was just about the toughest game warden I ever knew.

His philosophy was simply, "There are no mitigating circumstances. If a person violates the law, he is to be prosecuted to the fullest limits of my ability to prosecute him and there are absolutely no exceptions!" It was a pretty good attitude for a law enforcement officer in a sense but, sometimes, there are situations that must be taken into consideration. That's simply applying the human, commonsense aspect of law enforcement.

Well, the two of us were up there in those Ohio River bottoms one morning and there was about two inches of snow on the ground. It was cold! There was a blue north wind blowing and it was down to about eighteen degrees. We were down there for one reason: looking for early shooters who couldn't wait for the legal shooting time thirty minutes before sunrise.

We stood there and saw a small flock of Canada geese get up. These bottoms are endless. They are flat and you can see across them forever. We saw this little flock of geese, there were about eighteen of them, and they swung down across the river bottom, flying about sixty yards high.

They were just beginning to climb when we heard one shot and the lead goose, a huge old gander, just folded cleanly in the air and down he came.

We were standing there behind some brush and it was just beginning to break light. I looked at my watch. "That's exactly twenty minutes early, twenty minutes until legal shooting time."

"Yea, that's right," replied Jenkins. "And just as soon as I get this cigarette lit, I'm going straight down there and write him a summons."

"Well," I agreed. "I think that's quite proper. Let's go!"

There was no way this man could escape, this early shooter. The bottoms were flat and frozen over, hard as concrete, and we could drive our patrol car anywhere we wanted to.

So we went out. We saw a figure get up and run to where this goose fell, pick it up, and then walk out to the road. We got there just about the same time he did.

In spite of the cold weather, he had on only a blue denim shirt, blue denim dungarees, and a thin jacket. He was cold. He was also only about fourteen years old.

He was absolutely frozen stiff, but he was holding tight to the biggest Canada goose I've ever seen. He was excited and trembling all over.

"Hey! Look at what I just killed!"

And I replied, "Well, I think that just might be the biggest goose I've ever seen!"

The boy explained excitedly. "I've been lying down here fer six straight mornings. Five mornings they didn't come over me. Yesterday, I watched real careful and I saw right where they passed over. I got right at that spot this morning and they flew directly over me."

I asked, "How long have you been down here, son?"

"I've been down here about two hours, I guess. I got down here way before daylight."

I looked over at my partner. "Well, Jenkins, here's your man." The state game warden was looking down at the ground, kicking at the frozen ground with his toe while the boy stood there shivering, holding his little old single-barrel shotgun with one hand and holding his big gander by the neck with the other.

Finally Jenkins said, "Son, do you have a watch?"

"No, sir, but I think I'm all right on that shooting time."

I didn't say a word, just watched Jenkins and this boy. I was really enjoying all this because this really stern and strong conservation officer was feeling very uncomfortable for maybe the first time in his career.

Jenkins kicked at the ground a couple of more times and then he said, "Well, come on and get in the car and we'll run you home. You'll be late for school."

So the boy got in our partrol car, dragging this huge wild goose in after him, a goose that was killed contrary to the Migratory Bird Treaty Act, and we hauled him up to his house, an old ramshackle farmhouse, and let him out.

After we had let the boy out and were proceeding on down in the bottoms, I broke a long silence finally. "Well, he violated the law. Why didn't you write him up?"

"Yea," Jenkins said. "I guess he did."

"Hell, there's no guesswork about it. He shot twenty minutes early, and that's a violation of the law! You've wrote people up almost every morning this week for the same violation."

"Well, I didn't write him."

"OK, you didn't write him."

The state game warden stared hard at me. I could tell he was getting a little riled up.

"Why the hell didn't *you* write him up, Parker?"

I replied, "Well, I had several reasons for not writing him up. Number one, his violation was unintentional. Number two, he's a juvenile. Number three, if ever a man earned a goose, that boy sure earned his. I didn't have any intentions of writing him up."

Jenkins was getting a little red in the face. "OK, OK, let's forget about it!"

"All right," I replied. But my partner was rather testy for the rest of the day.

Well, about a week later, I was down in those river bottoms alone one day and about seven o'clock in the morning, I guess, I saw a fellow get up from a little ol' corn-shock blind and come out to the road.

So I eased on down the road to check him out and it was the same young lad wearing the same clothes.

"Did you do any good this morning?"

"No, I didn't get a shot."

Then with great pride, he turned back the sleeve on his dungaree jacket and he said, "Well, I guess I'd better be going. I don't want to be late for school." There, on his wrist, was a brand-new Timex watch.

I said, "Son that's a very fine watch you have there."

"Yes, sir! I'm very proud of it. It's a good one."

"Where did you get such a nice watch?"

"That game warden gave it to me."

"You mean Mr. Jenkins?"

"Yes, sir." Then the boy told me the story. "You know that same night after I killed that big goose down there?"

"Yea."

"Well, Mr. Jenkins came by the house that night about seven-thirty and put a small package in Ma's hand. 'Give that to the boy,' he said. 'Also give him this hunting regulations booklet. This is the marked shooting schedule. He can't shoot before this time and he can't shoot after this time, according to the changing of sunrise and sunset.' Then Mr. Jenkins turned and left the house."

I could see that the boy was extremely proud of that watch. Well, this literally tickled me to death. I couldn't wait until I got back to Henderson.

I got there about nine-thirty or ten A.M. and saw Jenkins's patrol car sitting in front of Farral's Restaurant and I stopped in for some coffee.

Jenkins was in there, sitting at the counter having coffee and I sat down beside him.

"How're you doing, Jenkins?"

"Fine, just fine."

"I saw that same little boy down in the bottom awhile ago."

"Oh? Did you? Was he hunting?"

"Yea, he sure was. He had a nice Timex watch, too."

Jenkins looked at me, feigning surprise. "He did?"

"Yea, he sure did."

"Well, that'll probably eliminate that early shooting, won't it?"

"Yes," I agreed, "in all probability it will."

So we just sat there and sipped our coffee for a few minutes and I finally asked, "How much did that damned watch cost you?"

"What watch?"

"The one you bought that little boy!"

"Why, I didn't buy him any watch!"

"The hell you didn't buy him that watch. He told me you did."

Jenkins looked sheepish. He was a big man and he leaned way over his coffee cup like he was trying to hide in it.

"Well, it cost me twelve dollars."

I dug into my pocket. "OK, here's six. I'll split it with you."

This incident gave me an insight into the character of this man. Donan Jenkins is like many of our conservation officers, both state and federal. They are dedicated and understanding. Some wear gray uniforms, some blue, some brown, and some wear no uniforms at all, but they form a thin line of protection to our wildlife resources that stretches across the North American continent, too thin a line for the job that has to be done.

Men like Jenkins deserve a hell of a lot more credit than they'll ever get.

chapter 11

Jacklighting Rabbits in Kentucky

THERE WAS QUITE a bit of jacklighting, hunting at night with the aid of a spotlight, going on in this Henderson County area. There were a few deer on old Camp Breckinridge and a few in other sections of both Henderson and Union counties of Kentucky. These were the prey of the jacklighters, but hunting rabbits at night was the major "sport."

Of course, this was contrary to the Kentucky game laws and I'd give the state wardens a hand at stopping this practice whenever I could.

Well, one night Donan Jenkins and I were up there in the country around Henderson checking out a complaint on nighttime rabbit shooting.

We got out into the area, typical farmland, about seven-thirty or eight o'clock one night, cruising along an old dirt road near a small country town called Spottsville, up where the Ohio River makes a big swing to the north.

I guess it was about nine o'clock when we heard a shot and we got out of the car and climbed a tall bank where we could see a good piece of the country with night binoculars.

We saw a car heading toward us on the same road we were on. It crossed a cattle guard and then turned off into a pasture field.

Well, we watched this jacklighter tour the field. It was very cold, the ground was frozen. A rabbit suddenly appeared in his head-lights. The car stopped. We saw the red fire from the muzzle of the man's shotgun; we saw the driver get out, pick up the rabbit, bring it back to his car, and throw it in the back. Then he continued touring the pasture field, trying to pick up another rabbit in his headlights.

And he was successful. He killed three more rabbits in the next twenty or thirty minutes.

I nudged Jenkins and said, "Just wait, now. He's got to come down this road. You get behind the point where he'll have to stop, and hide in the brush. I'll get this patrol car around the curve where he can't see me and block the road. When he comes, I'll turn on the headlights and the red blinker and you grab him before he can make a run for it."

Well, Donan got out and concealed himself in the hedgerow and the fellow did come down the road our way.

When he came around the curve, at the minute his headlights hit the patrol car, I turned on the headlights and the flashing red dome light and jumped out of the car.

As I approached the car on one side and Donan on the other, this fellow, he must have been six feet tall and real thin, dressed in coveralls, jumped out of the car and starting calling, "Here! Here! Here!"

He looked at us and said, "Hey, fellows, have you seen my dog?"

Well, I got rather amused. This was one approach that I had never heard in my entire life!

"No, I haven't," I said. "Have you lost a dog?"

"Hell, yes, I've lost a dog and I mean a real valuable dog! Man, I've been driving these roads all afternoon and all night, shooting off my gun and calling that dog. That damned dog is worth two hundred and fifty dollars and what's worse, I just got him on trial."

Well, this was just about the funniest thing I had ever heard in my life! Talk about a man with a built-in alibi! He really had one!

"That's great," I said. "I certainly hope you find that dog. In fact, I would help you in any way I could, but I am a federal game warden and this man standing behind you is a state game warden and those four rabbits he has in his hand, he just took off the floorboard in the back of your car."

I continued. "He's also got in his hand a shotgun, looks like a single-barrel four-ten shotgun that you threw out of the right-hand window of your car when I turned the red lights on."

The guy said, "Well, that does it. That sure does it! My daddy and I went rabbit hunting this afternoon and we killed those damned rabbits. We got back to the house about five-thirty and the old man said, 'Come on in, son, and let's clean those rabbits and eat some supper and you can go back later and look for that dog.'

"But I said, 'Nope, Dad, I'm going to hit the road again. I can't eat or sleep until I find that dog. I'm going to start driving and calling that dog and shooting my gun off and maybe he'll come to me.'

"Dad done told me, 'Well, son, you go right ahead, but you'd better take them rabbits out of that car, because if a game warden sees you riding along, shooting your gun off and stepping out and yelling and everything, he'll think that you're shooting rabbits at night.' "

Well, this nearly threw me into convulsions. I thought, "This is the greatest story I've ever heard from a lawbreaker and I've heard a lot."

I told this country boy who looked like a beanpole, "Well, the rabbits are warm. They are freshly killed and it's rather late. It's been dark now for about four hours and rigor mortis sets in pretty quick at this time of year, especially when it's as cold as it is."

He's got one for that, too. "Yea, it's that old transmission in the car. You go in and put your hands on that floorboard and feel it. It's so damn warm that it spoils everything I put back there. I guarantee them rabbits have been lying right there since about three-thirty this afternoon."

"Look," I said, "we watched you kill those rabbits out in that pasture field there, so you can just get off that dog-calling kick or that dog-looking kick or whatever damned kick it is that you're on. You are violating a state game law and we are going to take some information from you and you are going to have to come into court."

Well, this six-feet-six country boy in his coveralls was silent for about a minute or so and then he started to cry. He was crying real tears.

I was astounded! He was somewhere around twenty or twenty-five years old.

"What's your problem?" I asked him.

"Just give me that gun back and one shell."

"What do you want with the gun and one shell?"

"Well, I'm going to get over here in the ditch and I won't be in anybody's way. I'm just going to go ahead and kill myself."

"Look!" I told him. "We're not going to give you the gun or the shells back. A man killing himself over being arrested for a petty offense, a misdemeanor, is a rather stupid thing to do, don't you think?"

"Well," he said, "this ain't the only trouble I'm in. I'm in real, serious trouble!"

"What kind of trouble?"

"I want to tell you. I was in Henderson last night, and I got drunk. Coming on back out, the state police got after me and I run 'em all over these river bottoms before they finally hemmed me down here next to the dam. I jumped out of the car, and I run 'em for about two or three hours before they caught me and when they did catch me, they were madder'n a damned hornet!

"They carried me up to Henderson and put me in jail and I didn't get out until nine o'clock this morning. I'm under a five-hundred-dollar bond."

"Well," I told the boy, "that's a serious matter, driving while intoxicated, but I don't think it's a good enough reason for a man to want to kill himself."

But the boy shook his head. "You don't know what else kind of trouble I'm in. I'm in some real bad trouble besides that!"

"What else is bothering you?" I asked.

"Well," he explained, "I've been going with an ol' gal who lives up around Spottsville, been going with her for about six months and I took her out every night and every night I tried to get into her pants but she say, 'Uh, uh . . . no way!' Night after night I kept tryin' and every night she kept saying no!

"Finally she said to me one night, 'You heard anything about these newfangled birth control pills they got now?'

" 'Yea, I've heard about them,' I told her.

" 'Well, you get us some of them pills at the drugstore and we'll just try that.'

"Hell," the rabbit shooter said, "the next morning I legged it up to Henderson. I couldn't wait for the drugstore to open. I went in and asked for some of them pills and found out that you got to have a prescription to get them. Hell, I couldn't get no damned prescription."

That tall young fellow we caught then asked Donan Jenkins and me, "You know those little red candy balls they use for cookin' apples, them little red cinnamon balls?"

"Yea."

"Well, I saw a crock full of them on the drugstore counter and I told the gal behind the counter, 'Gimme a nickle's worth of them cinnamon balls.'

"She gave me about thirty of them, I reckon, and I went on home and found one of them little plastic prescription jars that medicine comes in and I put them candy balls in that.

"That night I took my gal out again. I was grinning all the way and when we got down to the dam, I told her, 'Look here what I got, Hon. You put one of them under your tongue and you hit the back seat!'

"Well, she did and just my damned luck, she come up pregnant!"

"Oh," I told the boy, "that's very bad."

"Yeah," he said, "it's bad all right. It's worse than you think. You don't know her father. Her father's the meanest son of a bitch in these bottoms. He's told me, done told me twice. If we ain't married when that baby comes, I'm a dead duck."

Then I said, "Look horse, you've got some time. A baby takes nine months."

But he only shook his head. "I ain't got no time a-tall. She's 'spectin' to drop jest any day!"

"You've really got a problem," I told him. "What time did the state police cite you into court?"

"I'm supposed to be over there before Judge Johnson tomorrow at three o'clock."

"Fine. You meet us at Judge Johnson's office at one o'clock."

He agreed to do this, so we took his gun and his rabbits and went on patrolling.

The next afternoon, at one o'clock, that boy dutifully appeared in Judge Johnson's chambers and we dutifully charged him with taking and attempting to take rabbits at night with a light in violation of the Kentucky game laws.

He entered a plea of "Not Guilty" and we had quite a lengthy little trial in which a lot of the excuses that he had given us the night before about looking for a dog came up again.

But after we presented the evidence, Judge Johnson found him guilty and fined him $250 and costs.

"Well," the boy said, "Judge, I ain't got any money."

"In that case," Judge Johnson replied, "Agent Parker, I'll write you a registration slip for Cleo Gish's 'hotel.' "

This ol' boy we'd caught rabbit hunting knew what this meant because he knew that Cleo Gish was the Henderson County jailer.

So the judge wrote us out a committing order and Jenkins and I put this Kentucky boy in the patrol car and took him off to jail. I was chuckling to myself because we had beaten the state police by a couple of hours.

On the way, the rabbit hunter looked at me and asked, "You're taking me to jail, ain't you?"

"Yes, that's where we're taking you."

"How long do I have to stay in there?"

"Well, under the Kentucky law, you get credit for two dollars a day. You have to pay two hundred and sixty-five dollars and that will amount to about a hundred and thirty days."

He was silent for a moment. "Well, Mr. Game Warden, I'll tell you one thing. I can't marry that ol' gal if I'm in jail, can I?"

"I don't know," I told him. "I really don't know about that."

Well, Donan and I carried the boy over to the Henderson County jail and they booked him and put him in a cell.

At that time, they did some strange things in Henderson County, Kentucky. I found out later that this girl's father came down to the jail, posted $265 in cash bond, and took this ol' boy out of jail. He took him away in a car, along with the girl he'd knocked up, and carried them to a nearby state that didn't require a waiting period and got them married.

Then he brought that boy right back to the jail and got his $265 back!

The girl's father left him there to serve out all his time, including the time that resulted from the charges the Kentucky State Police later placed on him. By the time he got out of there, he was older, wiser, and married!

But waterfowl, not rabbits, were my main concern while I was in Kentucky.

chapter 12

Outlaw Boat Races on the Ohio River

I WAS WORKING a small boat on the Ohio River in those days and had a terrible problem with motorboats because everybody up there had a more powerful, faster boat than I did. For every one violator of the Migratory Bird Treaty Act I caught, ten got away.

So I contacted Bill Davis, regional supervisor down in Atlanta, and told him my problem. "Bill, I've got to have a larger and faster boat up here to get this job done that needs to be done." He agreed.

As a result, I bought a fifteen-foot runabout and equipped it with a 700 Mercury outboard engine. This outfit could do forty miles an hour if it had to.

During the winter of 1961 and 1962, I tackled the biggest problem we had on that stretch of the Ohio River and that was shooting out of a fast-moving motorboat. This type of violation ranged from Paducah, Kentucky, to Cincinnati, Ohio, and that's one hell of a long stretch of water, approximately 250 miles!

They were so much faster that all I got was somebody standing up in the stern of the offending outboard motorboat, thumbing his nose at me as they went around a bend.

But with the new equipment, the odds were in my favor. This new boat and the seventy-horsepower motor was so fast that it was frightening. It was the fastest damned boat I have ever been in.

I couldn't wait for the duck season of 1962 to open and when it did open, I let this new boat be seen on the river as little as possible. This was the only year they made that powerful Mercury engine and I never dared open it up in public. When I was sure that nobody was around, I would test 'er out at full throttle, but when I was being watched, I would only run her at about twenty or twenty-five knots.

We had a little rise on the Ohio River that year at about the last of November or the early part of December and when the river rises, the ducks go to the willows along the banks to escape the swift waters and that's when the violators would kill the hell out of them.

Time after time after time, after the season really got under way, I would leave Henderson around three o'clock in the morning and run thirty to thirty-five miles of river. I never worked close to where I left my car because they quickly associated me with that patrol car. The section where I left the car would usually take care of itself. They thought I was in the area and things were relatively quiet for that reason.

I would go to a distant part of the river and hide the damned boat in the willows and I would set there and drink coffee and wait. I knew that if I waited long enough, the duck killers would come. I would always pick a good section of the river that the ducks frequented.

On good days, I would nail a couple of bunches of motorboat shooters. They would come around the bend with those high-powered inboards and outboards and they would come around the corners shooting ducks and dipping them up out of the river with a big dip net.

Then's when I would come out from the willows and usually they'd see me and the race was on. There would be a couple of them in the boat, and they'd be watching for drift—usually there is quite a bit of drift (debris) in the river when it is on the rise and that stuff makes it dangerous to run at high speed.

Once in a while, they'd look around to see where I was and the first time they looked I'd be about a half mile behind them, but the next time they looked for me, I was quite often crossing their wake and setting alongside.

I'd cut my motor down to their speed and shout over to them, "Shut it off!" This would always put them in a state of shock.

But there were a few instances that tickled the hell out of me.

There was a fellow by the name of John Driscoll who worked for the city of Smithland right down there at the confluence of the Ohio and Cumberland rivers. John was pretty bad about shooting ducks from a motorboat. He'd tell people all up and down the river that he really enjoyed this "sport" and that nobody was going to stop him.

I noted that if I launched at Smithland, very often I would work that section of the river for several days and not see a thing.

Yet, I kept getting reports of motorboat shooting in the area. So I launched early one morning at a little place in Union County just below Shawneetown, Illinois, and I ran forty-five miles of river to get to the section where John Driscoll boat-hunted.

I backed into the willows this morning and it was a bad day. It was sleeting; very bad weather-but a damned good day for the motorboat shooters.

About nine-thirty, I saw ol' John coming around the bend, he and his hunting companion. John was riding shotgun and the other fellow was running the boat.

They socked it to a couple of black ducks straight across from where I was hiding. I let them get almost to where the river swept into a right-hand turn—they were working the right bank—and then I tooled this seventy-horse outboard up, went across the river and fell in behind them.

They had a very fast outfit, so they felt completely secure.

I came around and got about fifty feet behind them and then just set there, staying with them. I had been following them for about a quarter of a mile, I guess, and suddenly there was five or six mallards come out of the willows. The shooters knocked three of them down and, as they circled to pick them up, there my boat set.

I have never seen such looks of consternation in my life. They tried to make a run for it and, with no trouble at all, I pulled alongside. In fact, I circled them and with them going at top speed this made it quite apparent that I could catch them.

They gave up.

"OK, John. Let's have the ducks."

"Now, Mr. Parker, we didn't kill all these from the motorboat."

"Well, John, it doesn't matter what you killed from the motorboat. I think that you are a little bit heavy, too. I think you have a few more birds than you should have. Put them over here in my boat, John. Put your guns in here too and I need some information. This type of hunting has got to cease."

After I got their names, addresses, license numbers, and the information I needed, I wrote them summonses and let them go.

"OK, John, you can go home now, but look, you've had a big mouth. You've run from Paducah to Henderson telling people how bad you were, violating the law with this motorboat and how fast your damn boat is and how many successful hunts you've had. Now I want you to make the same damn stops and tell them what's happened to you today."

All he could do was swallow.

Well, late that night I got back into where I had launched my boat and guess who was sitting there on my trailer, waiting for me? John Driscoll! He had looked the river up and down until he had found where I had put in.

"Good evening, John."

"Can I help you load your boat, Mr. Parker?"

"No thanks, it's rigged for a one-man operation, no problem whatsoever."

"Mr. Parker, how much is this trouble I'm in going to cost me?"

"John, I am not part of the federal judicial system and I can't tell you. I don't know what it is going to cost you, but I certainly hope that it is enough to get your attention. I promise you one thing. It *is* going to cost you!"

"Mr. Parker, when do you think this case will come up?"

"Really, John, I don't know when it will come up. But you can depend on it coming up sooner or later, that's for sure. The process is that when I have the time I have to file a written report with the United States attorney who, when he has the time, files the case with the court, and when the court has the time, they will schedule it for trial."

I could tell by looking at him that he was really disturbed about this situation and I thought that this might be the opportunity to cure him once and for all, rather than just give him a little dose of it. I just might be able to administer lifetime immunization to such unlawful actions that he had been engaged in. I really poured it on him, telling him about the due process of the law and what might happen to him.

From then on, every time I launched my boat from Paducah, Kentucky, to Shawneetown, Illinois, and spent the day on the river, John Driscoll would find the place where I launched and he'd be there waiting when I pulled in at night. This went on for the next four or five weeks. He'd be there sitting on my boat trailer. Some days he must have waited at least a half of the day there.

One afternoon, just before Christmas of 1962, I had launched at Smithland, which was right near where John lived. I came back in after a while and there he was, as usual, sitting on the boat trailer.

He looked very pale. "Mr. Parker, can I talk to you?"

"Certainly, John. I'm a public servant and anything I can do to help you, I would be happy to do."

"Mr. Parker," he said, "I can't eat, I can't sleep, and with all these people around here talking about me going to jail and all that, why it's driving me crazy. I've got to get rid of it. I just can't live with it. I can't carry it anymore. I've got to know what's going to happen!"

And I thought, "Well, he's had five weeks of it and that's just about enough."

I said, "John, I see that you are suffering from being under the strain of this and I'll try to speed it up. But do you know what's going to happen to you if I ever catch you again?"

"What?"

"The procedure would be," I answered, "that whatever you are doing, I'd handcuff you and I'd take you to the nearest United States commissioner, where you would be committed to bond if we happened to get there during the time that the United States commissioner was in session. Otherwise, I'd have to put you in jail until nine o'clock the next morning. That's the way I'll handle it in the future."

He looked sick. "Mr. Parker, there'll be no future. I'll swear to that, if you can only get me off of this one!"

"There is no getting off of this one, John."

"I don't mean that," he stammered. "Just take me to court and set a fine and let me get it off my back!"

That same night, Warden Hack Chambliss called me. "Bill, if you don't hurry up and terminate that case against old John Driscoll, he is going to end up in a mental institution. He's got the whole county worried about him."

I answered, "Do you think he's had enough?"

Hack replied, "Hell, man, he's cured."

"OK, Hack, will you go down there and tell John that if he wants to go before the judge and enter a plea of guilty to killing three wild ducks from a motorboat and pay a hundred and costs on each charge, he can this time, but next time it's going to be very bad."

You know, I believe, to this day, John has never put another shotgun in a motorboat.

The word spread, and I literally tore hell out of the motorboat shooting on that section of the Ohio. I scared the hell out of them because they never knew where or when I would appear and they knew that I had the fastest damn boat on the river.

chapter 13

The Lonesome Goose

ONE AFTERNOON, DONAN JENKINS and I had stopped our boat right in the middle of the Wabash River. It was about three-thirty or maybe four o'clock and we had pulled over into an eddy to make a pot of coffee. We had a little gas stove aboard. The weather was bitter cold.

As we sat there drinking our coffee, Jenkins pointed up the river, "Nine geese heading this way," he said. They were coming down the river, flying about 150 yards high. They came right over Wabash Island and then we heard nine or possibly a dozen shots.

I shook my head. "There you are, Jenkins. Typical goose hunters who think that the damned geese are right on top of their guns." Skybusters is what we call these shooters who try to bring down a bird that is completely out of range.

Well, Donan and I watched the geese. They kept coming on down the river, but it was apparent that one of the geese was in difficulty. He fell behind the others by about twenty yards.

"Watch those geese," I told him. "One of them is hurt."

We focused our glasses on this goose, an old gander, and watched him as he desperately kept up with the rest of the flock, but it only lasted a couple of minutes. Suddenly, he set his wings and came down toward the river. At the same time, another goose peeled out of the flock and came to the river with him.

Well, we watched that wounded goose closely. He banked into the wind and came in to land on the water but collapsed about ten feet above the water and fell, I am sure, quite dead into the river.

The other goose immediately set right down beside this dead gander.

We cranked up the motor.

"Donan, that's amazing! They must be a mated pair."

"Well, I guess they are," Jenkins said. "I've heard that they will do that, watch out for each other."

"Yes," I answered. "Many times I've seen them. A flock will come in and several geese will be killed out of that flock and you will see one or two birds peel out of the flight and come right back into the blind and they are generally killed, too. These are the mated pairs. A wild Canada goose won't abandon its mate."

We went on downriver to where these two geese were and we witnessed one of the most amazing things that I have ever seen. Few people have ever had the same opportunity.

The live goose was swimming against the current, trying to push the body of her dead mate to a nearby sandbar. The gander's head was limp and I was sure that the bird was stone dead, but the female goose kept running her head and neck under her mate's neck, trying to raise his head out of the water.

Well, in a few minutes, she had managed to shove the gander in to shore and the wake from our boat swept the dead bird up on the edge of the beach. His mate paid little attention to us. She stood by her dead mate and she was making sounds I had never before heard a goose make. You might call it a sort of whisper, a low-keyed, muted "honk" that came from somewhere deep inside her. We got within twenty feet of her with the boat and she made no effort to leave.

I nudged my partner. "This is really something. That's pure devotion, natural devotion in a wild creature." I was stunned by the tragic sight.

Well, about the time we edged the boat into the sandbar, she launched into flight. We picked up the body of the dead gander and put it in the boat and all this time, his mate circled us at about 150 feet high. She stayed with us for five or ten minutes and then she started flying down the river.

We went on down to Shawneetown landing and started to take the boat up, and after we shut the motor off I could hear this goose calling, calling. She was flying back and forth from Shawneetown to Wabash Island and she was calling every time her wings beat.

We dressed and sexed this dead goose there by the landing. It was an old gander, probably had been mated for a long time. It would eventually go to the Henderson County Home for the Aged and not be wasted.

It was getting late by this time, so Donan and I decided that we would go into Shawneetown. There was a little riverside diner there that had some of the finest catfish and hush puppies that a man ever bit into. We'd have us a big catfish dinner and try to forget the sad thing we had just witnessed.

By the time we came back to pick up the boat and load it on the trailer, it was about nine P.M. and the minute we got out of the car, we could hear this lonesome goose flying and calling. At least it was *a* goose flying and calling from Shawneetown Bridge all the way to Wabash Island. She was calling every time her wings beat and she was flying low.

Jenkins shrugged. "You know, that gives me the strangest feeling, Bill." I agreed.

We made arrangements to meet early the next morning, at four o'clock as a matter of fact, and work the same section of the river for early shooters.

So I met Jenkins the next day and we had an early breakfast together and then we went on down to the Shawneetown Bridge. We decided to drop off the boat, leave it on the trailer, and drive up the middle of the river bottom to keep our eye on seven or eight blinds we knew about. We would be in a good position in case there was early shooting from any of these blinds.

So we drove up the bottom and parked the patrol car. It was just before dawn and amazingly, there was a goose flying, flying some two hundred yards high from Wabash Island to the Shawneetown Bridge and back, calling constantly in rhythm to the beatings of her wings.

It gave me one hell of an eerie feeling; the short hairs stood up on the back of my neck.

It was beginning to get daylight and I could see this goose through the glasses. I also saw two hunters over on a sandbar on the Illinois side of the river.

They had put out about fifty decoys and were building a little brush blind around an old log over there.

"Watch this," I whispered, although there was no reason to keep my voice down. "The first pass that goose makes up that river, and the first call those hunters make on their goose caller, she's gone!"

We had already assumed that this goose was the mate of the one that had been killed the day before.

Well, those fellows had finished their blind just about shooting time. We saw them run and get into that blind and we knew that they had heard her as the goose was making one more turn up the river on her lonesome vigil.

We heard the mouth call from those hunters, "Honk, Honk, Honk" and she did too. At the very first note, she zeroed in on that sound. She locked her wings and glided in toward that blind and those wings never moved again. She went straight to that call, she never hesitated, and of course they killed her.

And I was sad, very sad all the rest of the day. We worked the entire patrol, each silent with our thoughts.

chapter 14

Pat the Retriever as a "Federal Agent"

PAT, MY LITTLE Labrador retriever, went with me wherever I went along the Ohio River. She had an extraordinary nose, she could find a duck or a goose that had been shot down, even three or four hours after it had been killed.

Time after time, I would encounter a hunter on one of those Ohio River sandbars where it was hard, cold hunting. And he'd say, "I shot a goose this morning and crippled it. Fell about a mile across the bottoms. I've been over there looking for it but couldn't find it. Could I take your dog over there and see if she can't find it for me?"

I would always say yes. Pat would work for anybody. Well, maybe forty-five minutes or maybe an hour later the hunter and Pat would come back and the goose would be with them.

Often Pat would trail a crippled bird that had hit the ground running, flush it from a brushpile, catch it, and bring it back to a hunter.

Well, she was a good friend to some of the goose hunters on the Ohio, but she was a feared enemy to other hunters. There was absolutely no way to hide migratory waterfowl in those Ohio River bottoms without Pat finding the illegal bird.

Pat made case after case for me. I was amazed at her performance. I trained her to hand signals. The minute we hit one of those Ohio River islands, I started checking hunters in the immediate vicinity of their blinds while Pat, at the same time, was inspecting all of the territory within seven hundred or so yards around that particular blind. She dug the hidden waterfowl out of the sand, she got illegal birds out of hollow logs. She was a very efficient "federal agent" and I'd always find a way to tie the illegal birds she had found to the hunters we were checking at the time. I don't recall ever losing a case that Pat made for me or helped me make.

On a sandbar above Wabash Island one morning about nine-thirty, I went in to check a blind. I had heard shooting, a hell of a lot of shooting coming from that area. It had been almost continuous since the start of legal shooting time early that morning. I had been working a section below this area and got to the scene of all this damn shooting about ten o'clock in the morning and three fellows were in this blind and I mean, that blind was ankle-deep in freshly fired shotgun shells.

So I walked up and introduced myself. "I'm Bill Parker, federal game warden. I want to have a look at your hunting credentials and check your guns." I asked them if they had had any luck.

"No," they replied. "We've had a very poor day."

"Well, you've certainly done a lot of shooting. I've heard a lot of shooting up this way this morning earlier, and you've got plenty of spent shells in your blind."

They agreed that they had done an abnormal amount of shooting, but they hadn't killed but three birds apiece. The limit was four.

Meanwhile, Pat was nosing around up in a patch of willows back of the blind about forty or fifty or so yards away and I waited and waited for her to report.

She couldn't find anything and finally she came back in for further instructions. I sent her out again. This time Pat was gone for about ten minutes and I couldn't find her. I went to the boat and got the whistle. (She was trained to it.) She still wouldn't come in. I waited for a few more minutes and then I blew the whistle again. This time she barked in answer. Well, I really set down on that whistle the next time and she knew from the way I blew that she had better respond in one way or another.

She barked more insistently this time, but she still didn't come in.

"Well, what in the hell is going on here?"

Then she started barking frantically in answer to the whistle.

"She must be hung up in a trap," I thought.

The three duck hunters were looking at each other by this time and I told them, "You gentlemen wait right here and I'll go over and see what seems to be bothering my Labrador."

So I walked over there to where she was and she was trying to climb this small tree. I looked up in the branches and got seventeen mallard ducks down that had been tied there. They were hanging higher than Pat could reach.

Well, I went back to the sandbar with all of these birds and said, "Gentlemen, all of these birds are freshly killed. I've carefully checked the other side of that willow grove and there are no fresh tracks coming from that direction. The tracks are all on this side. Is there anything that you want to tell me?"

One of them finally spoke up, "I guess that it's pretty apparent that we killed those birds."

"Yes," I agreed. "And it's also apparent that you are quite a few ducks over the limit."

"I guess we are," the fellow replied. "The only thing that distresses me about this thing is that I really hate to be caught by a damned dog!"

"Well," I said, "she's not just any kind of a dog. She's kinda special!"

Pat would spend the entire day with me in a cold boat, running at high speed on that Ohio River at temperatures that were often well below freezing. She enjoyed it. She really enjoyed it! And after a hard day's work, she would curl up in the car and go to sleep. She was a distinct pleasure to travel with. She never caused any trouble, and she was my constant companion for some eight or eight and a half years.

Pat had an extremely soft and tender mouth. She caught thousands of young ducklings for me in the springtime of the year when I would sex them, band them, and release them.

I worked Pat on the small rivers in Kentucky during May and June, and she was especially good on wood ducks. The Tradewater River up there in Webster County, Kentucky, was one of the finest wood duck areas that I have ever worked. We found literally hundreds of wood ducks on that river and one afternoon, as Pat and I were coming down the Tradewater, a remarkable thing happened.

The river was rather narrow and the ducks would go out ahead of our canoe. Pat could smell those ducks when they hid on the banks and she'd let me know that they were there.

When she'd smell 'em, she'd whine and when she'd whine, I'd immediately put her out on the bank and she'd start working. If there were ducks there, she'd have one shortly and bring it back to me.

She brought one back once that couldn't have been out of the egg for more than two or three days. It was a tiny little thing and I thought that maybe Pat had injured it. She kinda spread the duckling out in my hand and it was wet and still.

"Well," I thought, "this little fellow is probably dead."

Then I could see that tiny eye. It was a black, beady eye and it was the only thing about that baby duck that had any movement to it at all. I decided that the duckling wasn't dead after all, so I set him down on a little mud flat next to the water and stepped back. He took off down that mud flat, hit the water, ran across the water for about six feet, and then went under, disappearing.

Well, I didn't want Pat handling three- or four-day old ducklings, but before I could get her away, she got the hen. This was most unusual because wood duck hens in their early stages of brooding are flight ducks, with their nests usually a hole in a hollow tree. They can and do fly.

But this hen couldn't fly. When Pat brought her to me, I noticed that one of her wings was gone, completely gone from her body. In fact, there was just a raised spot there where the wing should have been. Perhaps the duck had been hatched that way.

I sat on that riverbank with this bird in my hand and wondered how she managed to survive the winter. "She's got to be at least one year old." She was, of course, flightless during the frozen winter months and this Tradewater River freezes over solid, so she's most fortunate to be alive and now she even has managed to raise a brood.

That meant that she had to nest on the ground. She certainly couldn't have nested like a normal wood duck in a hollow tree. She couldn't fly and she surely couldn't climb!

I thought about banding her, but then I had second thoughts.

"No, it would be pointless to put a band on her. There's no way she can go anywhere on one wing. All she can do is walk!"

So I released her and, well, I thought a lot about her. It was one of those oddities of nature.

The next spring, I guess about the middle of May, Pat and I were catching and banding ducks within two hundred yards of the same place. We came around a bend in the river and two half-grown wood ducks ran out of the water and up the bank.

I put Pat out at the spot where the ducks had left the river and I got out my net and bag that I kept the ducks in until I had banded them.

Pat brought me seven half-grown wood ducks and I put 'em in this nylon-mesh bag. The next time she came back, Pat had a duck hen and I happened to think about the one-winged hen that I had found in just about this same spot the spring before.

When Pat delivered this duck, lo and behold, this too was a wood duck with only one wing! For the life of me, I couldn't recall whether the duck of the previous year was missing the right or left wing, so I couldn't swear that this was the same duck. I like to think, though, that she had been able to survive three hard winters on the Tradewater River and had raised two fine broods. This with only one wing!

One time in late May when I was banding wood ducks on the Tradewater River, I had traveled all the way to the head of the river. This was one of the wildest sections of Webster County, Kentucky, hilly and remote. I don't think that there was a house within five miles of where I was working. As usual, Pat was with me in the canoe and way the heck up there along a huge bluff we ran a brood of wood ducks out. Pat was catching them for me. I didn't have my holding bag at the time, had left it in the canoe, so I was dropping these half-grown wood ducks in the game pocket of my canvas hunting coat.

I had worn the coat because, in that country in late May, the mosquitoes would eat you alive if you didn't wear some sort of protective clothing.

Pat had brought me about six of those ducklings and was looking for the rest of the brood when suddenly I heard a voice that seemed to come out of nowhere.

"Ain't them damned ducks too little fer eatin'?"

Well, I froze. I looked in the direction where I thought the voice had come from and up on the top of that high bluff above me, there stood a young man, maybe twenty years old. He had on a pair of blue jeans and those rolled up high around his legs. He was barefoot, no shirt, sunburned, tousle-headed. He just stood there, looking down at me.

He repeated his question. "Ain't them damned ducks too little fer eatin'?"

"Why, I don't plan to eat them."

"Well, what are you doin' with 'em then?"

"Come on down here and I'll show you."

He came down off that high bluff just like a mountain goat. He got down on the riverbank to where I was and I noticed that he was covered with mosquitoes. They were very bad but he paid no attention to them whatsoever. There must have been a thousand of them eating on him at one time.

I explained to him why we were banding the birds, so that we could study their migration patterns and habits. I showed him how to sex the ducks as to whether they were male or female and I told him a little bit about the migrational habits of waterfowl.

"Now these wood ducks will probably leave this area in early September and might go as far north as Michigan where they would stage up for their fall migration south. According to our banding records, most of them will winter in Florida."

Well, this backwoods boy was absolutely amazed at all of this and I was equally amazed at his resistance to those mosquitoes that seemed to be eating him alive.

"Son, how do you stand those damned mosquitoes? Aren't they bothering you?"

"Naw, you git used to 'em after a while. I was born and raised here."

During my stay in Kentucky and particularly around Henderson, I related to these people with their simple, unaffected way of life, and especially to those who lived on the Ohio River in their homemade houseboats.

These were the "river rats" and the "hillbillies" who did not conform to the laws and conditions dictated by society. It was amazing to hear them talk, to tell of things that they witnessed in the course of their everyday life. These were the sights and sounds of the wilderness that most people don't experience in a lifetime. Things like watching a brood of young wood ducks coming out of a hole in a hollow tree that was often fifty or sixty feet above the ground. Things like watching a wild mink working along a remote mountain stream or like seeing fox squirrels at play.

But perhaps my most pleasant experience during that tour of Kentucky, which lasted from 1960 to 1966, was working with Pat, my Labrador retriever. During those summer months I took her to Canada to the great waterfowl nesting grounds of the western provinces to band ducks.

All of my experiences in Kentucky, however, did not end pleasantly or cast me in the role of a winner. The Ohio River was the principal area of operation, a battleground against the violators of the Federal Game and Fish Laws. Sometimes the Ohio River was the winner.

chapter 15

Flood Stage on the Ohio

THE OHIO RIVER, especially when it reaches the flood stage, is one of the most vicious rivers that I have ever worked. The currents are unbelievable. I've seen cottonwood trees float down the Ohio when it was angry, hit an eddy with a whirlpool and literally stand straight up in the air as if they were still rooted and then suddenly disappear.

This river was particularly dangerous when there was ice floating on it, yet during these winter months, the Ohio was used by waterfowlers for almost its entire length.

There is no doubt about it, the Ohio has always been a dangerous, treacherous stream.

It was on Christmas Eve of 1964 that I put my boat in there at the old Shawneetown Bridge early in the morning. It was a very unusual day. That morning, when I left my house, it was actually hot, very hot for that time of year. It must have been around seventy degrees.

But by the time I launched my boat at daylight, the thermometer had dropped to around fifty degrees. For some strange reason, the weather became erratic and most unusual. First it was warm, then cool. The wind blew with a fierceness that I had never seen before. It was almost a gale and it was variable. It came from all directions.

Then, about ten o'clock in the morning, the wind moved to the northwest. She was blowing steady and she was blowing strong.

The river was bank full, maybe a little over bank full, and the current was moving fast, very fast. Those sections where the wind was bucking the current were about the roughest stretches of water I have ever seen. I hugged the Illinois bank on the way upstream, running a fifty-horsepower outboard on a small Crosby Sea Sled.

Upstream I ran into a couple of waterfowlers who were hugging the willows. The two were friends of mine: one, C. D. Henry, a state police detective, and the other, a dentist, Dr. Higginson from Morgantown.

I pulled alongside and stopped to chat with them for a while. They had a small boat powered with a five-horse outboard. But they had been using oars and they had killed two ducks.

We shared some hot chocolate while hanging onto the edge of the willows. We talked for about twenty minutes and then I left.

"Be very careful, fellows. The river is extremely treacherous today, the weather is unsettled and I really don't know what to expect." Of course, they assured me that they would be careful.

I went on my patrol, working the rest of the day on the river, worked the Ohio all the way to Henderson and on back down to Shawneetown where I pulled my boat out just before sundown.

This being Christmas Eve, I got on home, took a good hot bath, and planned to spend the rest of the evening with my family, but things didn't work out that way.

About seven o'clock, the telephone rang.

It was a conservation officer down in Uniontown, Kentucky. "Have you checked those two hunters upriver today, Bill?"

"Yes, I did check them this morning."

"Where did you run into them?"

"About a mile above the Shawneetown Bridge, I guess, on the Illinois shore."

"Well, I'm concerned about them. They haven't come in as yet."

It was several hours past dark by then.

"Well, they did tell me that they were going to float down to a landing below Shawneetown. They left a car down there."

"Yes," Captain Mauzy replied, "I found that car there. I also found the car they left up at the other end of Wabash Island where they launched. But I haven't found them!"

"OK," I said, "I'll hook up the boat and I'll be right on down there."

By this time it was really turning cold. It had begun to sleet and snow, with the wind still holding northwest, and it was now blowing a real gale.

Well, I became real concerned about these two hunters while I was getting dressed. I knew that it was going to be a long night, so I put on a lot of warm clothes, got a quart of hot coffee in my patrol car, turned the red light on, and met Mauzy at Shawneetown Bridge in just a few minutes.

We launched from there and I think that it was the wildest night I have ever seen. We had packed the boat, a runabout fourteen feet long and six wide, with our gear and tried to launch it. By this time a considerable crowd had gathered, but there were no volunteers who offered to go out on the river with us on that wild night.

We had a high-powered spotlight on that boat and I took along a shotgun, shells, and a flashlight. We knew if these people had gone into the water and were wet, with the temperature dropping the way it was, way below freezing, they could not possibly survive the night.

We did know that these two hunters would habitually float down a stretch of river and if they killed a duck or so, then they'd swing to the other side of the river, put their motor on, run five or six miles back up, and then float down again.

We had no idea where to begin looking for them, so we decided to start on the lower end of Wabash Island and search as far down as we thought necessary and hopefully find them.

I think it was the wildest, stormiest night I can remember. We would stop periodically and fire three shots from a twelve-gauge pump gun. Then we'd load and fire three more and the wind would whip the sound away from the gun barrel. It was an eerie sound and unusual to see the flame from the gunfire crook and bend under the force of the wind.

Well, we bailed just about all night to keep ourselves afloat. The river was very high and rough and we took on a lot of water.

About two o'clock in the morning we were a half mile above Shawneetown on the north end of Bell Island and just a short distance below the point where I had stopped to talk to those men the morning before!

Suddenly, I noticed an object floating in the heavy surf against a sandbar over on the Illinois shore. I pulled the boat in, nosed it against the bank, and had Mauzy hold her fast while I got out to determine just what this object was.

When I put the flashlight on the object I still couldn't make it out plainly with all of the sleet and snow. I had the most eerie feeling when I walked down that sandbar. I discovered that it was a gasoline can, a red gasoline can, and I knew that the two people we were searching for had a can like it. I picked it up out of the water and set it further on the beach, and continued my search.

I found a bobber with a set of car keys drifting in against the beach. I picked that up and continued on down the bar. Just below that, I found an oar; then I found a gun case, and it then became apparent to me that these two men we were searching for were in the Ohio River.

Shortly later, I found what convinced me beyond any doubt that they were in the river and the matter of their survival was highly questionable.

I found a hip boot that had drifted in to the edge of the shore.

I gathered all of this stuff up and made my way back to the boat. There was still a shred of hope that they could have made it to shore and survived.

But, in that case, with the weather being what it was, we should make an immediate search downstream and see if we could locate them hanging on the willows or a drift.

We continued our sweep downstream, passed the Shawneetown Bridge, and went on down to a bar right at the mouth of the Saline River.

Now this was some five miles south of where we believed they had capsized, where we had found the debris from their boat, indicating a calamity of some sort.

We searched the north bank of that wild Ohio River very thoroughly, running close to the bank, and we were still discharging the shotgun periodically, hoping against hope for an answer. We were also using our voices, calling for these two people.

There are two islands in the middle of the Ohio just north of where the Saline enters the larger river. We searched those islands very closely. We even searched them for footprints, but found nothing.

Our search for these two men went on all night and the next morning, Christmas morning, and about four-thirty or five o'clock we pulled into the Shawneetown landing.

During this entire night we had the river solely to ourselves. No one else would go out on the Ohio in that weather, even though we desperately needed at least two boats to make a complete search.

Whatever had happened could have happened over a span of river that was too vast for one boat to investigate. But nobody would launch with us. That night the Ohio was too bad, too dangerous. But my experience in dealing with violent situations is that the real danger is losing control of the ability to control one's self.

Well, we spent the entire night on that river and it was a terrible night for the two of us.

The next morning, when we pulled into Shawneetown landing, there must have been 150 cars there and probably 250 people. Long before Captain Mauzy and I had come into the landing, we could see the fires they had built to withstand the cold.

When we docked, we saw that the Kentucky Department of Water Resources, or whatever it is that they call that outfit, was there with a big cruiser that was still waiting for dawn. The cruiser was there when we launched the night before. It was something like a twenty-four footer with an inboard motor and much more capable of that rough water we worked that night with our fourteen-foot runabout.

Well, we pulled into that landing, and I never will forget that crowd that was waiting. Everyone was very grim and solemn. It was a very trying time, Christmas morning, and Dr. Higginson had, I believe, seven children. I am sure that he had made great preparations for Christmas, so it was a very sad time for that family. Both of these men—the state policeman C. D. Henry, as well as Dr. Higginson—were very popular in the community and the entire community was assembled there on the riverbank waiting for us.

My own wife, Faye, was as worried as the rest, for there was no guarantee that we would return from our dangerous mission, either.

I never will forget the utter despair from that crowd, the groan that was universal, as we came ashore carrying a hip boot, an empty gun case, an oar, and a Johnson gas tank.

As if with one voice they asked us, "Is this what you found?"

"Yes."

"What do you think?"

"I fear the worst," I told them. "We found no trace of the boat and we found no trace of them. But the things that we did find lead me to believe that they are in the river and it is very doubtful that they could have survived after capsizing in a night as rough as last night."

They asked me, "Are you going to continue the search?"

And I told them, "I would like to be able to, but I am afraid the search is futile. I began my work yesterday morning at three-thirty and it is well past three-thirty now, so that is twenty-four hours that I have been without sleep or much food. If I thought that there was the slimmest chance that either of those men could have survived, I would spend as much time as necessary to find them, but now I am discontinuing the search and I will leave the recovery of the bodies up to you people."

And I left. It was a very sad Christmas.

Later that day, they launched several boats and the search continued for about five weeks. They drug every inch of the Ohio River that they could drag. All the way from the upper end of Bell Island down to the mouth of the Saline River where it enters the Ohio.

They never found anything. It was a most unusual situation.

I got back to my own home about nine o'clock Christmas morning and I slept through until the next morning at four o'clock, and then I went back to work.

But I thought about these two friends of mine a lot.

Doc Higginson practiced in the Union County seat of Morgantown and, as I said, he had a large family and was very popular.

He had quite a lot of insurance, but I understood at the time that when a person completely disappears, he cannot be declared legally dead for seven years, unless some reasonable evidence that he is dead is presented.

Well, a month after the accident, I had to appear before a coroner's jury that was set at Morgantown. I spent two hours before this jury, giving them the benefit of my experience with the Ohio River, with that type of operation the two men were engaged in relative to duck hunting, and with both of the people who were involved in the calamity.

It was amazing! The people in the community presented the insurance company with a surety bond in the amount of the insurance policies that he had, which were quite substantial.

It's not likely that their boat sunk. It was a well-built aluminum craft with buoyancy tanks built into it.

In all probability, a string of barges was coming down the river at a high rate of speed because of the flood stage. These barges are awesome things with six- or eight-foot screws on them. They chew up logs, debris, anything they hit.

These two duck hunters must have been surprised by some barges as they came around a bend. I don't believe the crew, because of the stormy conditions that day, were aware that they had hit anything.

C. D. Henry's body was found one year later, two hundred yards below where I found the gas tank. Dr. Higginson's body was never found.

chapter 16

Working the Waterfowl Nesting Grounds of Canada

DURING THE LATE fifties and early sixties, I was to spend much of my summers in the Saskatchewan Province of Canada catching young ducks that were still capable of flight, banding and sexing them. The spirit of cooperation between Canada and the United States in the area of conservation has been the one factor above all others that has maintained the wild duck population, waterfowl that recognizes neither geographical nor political boundaries. This cooperation must continue if our waterfowl are to survive.

Saskatchewan is pothole country—Canadian prairie land with wild bush country to the north and great stretches of wheatland in the southern end of the province, huge wheat fields dotted by potholes. The potholes, left from the glaciers, are ideal nesting sites for waterfowl, principally wild ducks of all species. This is the area that most of our ducks come from, especially the mallards that follow the Mississippi and Atlantic flyways.

We would use Labrador retrievers and our procedure was that we'd work a pothole, run the young ducks up on land. The hen duck was usually with the brood. She would flop around and try to distract the dog, but a well-trained Labrador would track the young ducks, pick up a duck, and bring it back to me uninjured. I'd put the duck in a bag and after we had caught the entire brood or even several broods, we'd sex them, age and band them and release them. This was done to study population, and breeding and migratory habits of the wild ducks.

Agent Harley Pierson, a short, active sort of fellow from down in Alabama, usually went with me on these trips. We were strangers in a strange land and much of the country was not thickly settled. Many of the farms had been abandoned, forsaken as homesteads, and the people had moved into Prince Albert where they could find more profitable work.

We rambled all over that country and when we found a promising pothole full of ducks, as most of them were, we usually wouldn't have to ask permission to catch the ducks because there would be no one on the farm. There were just weather-beaten, ramshackled buildings and maybe some rusting farm machinery left behind.

The first year we went up there, we took a huge Labrador named Smokey. Smokey was owned by Sumner Dow, a friend of mine from Nashville, Tennessee. The dog was an excellent hunter, about 125 or so pounds of active Labrador. He was the biggest Lab that I'd ever seen and when I picked him up, his owner said, "Now, Bill, you ration what he eats because he's a pig and he'll kill himself eating! He's got a thing about eating. He'll go right on through a twenty-five-pound sack of food if you make it available to him."

So I said, "OK, I'll be careful about his diet and see that Smokey is not overfed."

Well, that year, Agent Pierson went along and he and Smokey had a personality clash the minute they saw each other. Harley just couldn't stand the dog, and the Labrador absolutely detested Harley. Now Smokey was very headstrong and hard to control. To sort of calm him down a little, I also took Pat, my own little Labrador. I thought that maybe Pat would be a good influence on Smokey.

We took the dogs up in a trailer that we pulled behind our patrol car. There was a lot of serious business to get done. We needed to catch from sixteen to eighteen hundred mallards while we were in Canada, besides working some other breeds of wild ducks.

The first pothole we worked, it became quite apparent that Smokey was just too aggressive to handle these young ducklings without hurting them. If they were bruised at all, they would die, and when Smokey happened to lay one of those big paws of his on a duck, that was it. He didn't have Pat's tender mouth, either. Pat wouldn't hurt anything.

This was summertime, and the afternoons were very hot on those Canadian prairies. We pulled up to this pothole on one of these especially hot afternoons and I told Harley, "Leave old Smokey in the car [we'd left the trailer in town that day], I'm going to take Pat and let her work this pothole alone."

So I turned Pat out in this big field where there were about seven young mallards fluttering and running around and the mother hen was flopping this way and that as they will do to distract an enemy from their ducklings.

Well, ol' Smokey was watching all of this activity from out of the window of the car and he got so damned excited that Harley had to sit in there with him to keep him quieted down. He also had to keep the windows rolled up or that big dog would have busted out of there in no time flat!

I looked over there once and saw Harley setting behind the wheel. The next time I looked, Smokey was behind the wheel and Harley was nowhere to be seen. Maybe Smokey was sitting on him!

After about twenty minutes of this, Harley let out a yell. "I'm letting this damned dog out of here!"

He turned old Smokey loose, and across that prairie that dog raced. He picked himself out a mallard hen and he chased that duck out of sight. Then he came back to the pothole and took on another hen and ran her about a half a mile. In forty-five minutes Smokey was completely exhausted by the heat and lay on his back panting, his paws waving in the air and his big tongue hanging out of the side of his mouth.

Well, Pat followed Smokey's example. She found out it was more fun to chase the hens than to simply pick up the young ducklings. I despaired of catching any ducks at all on this trip and knew that some drastic measures were needed.

We were keeping our dogs at the home of a French Canadian, Pete Masurak, over in Prince Albert, so after that one bad experience, I kept Smokey tied up in Pete's yard and worked Pat alone, the next day.

At the first pothole, she chased three hens and realized that there was no way she could catch them. When I called her back on the whistle, she started working the young ducks on her own and handled them flawlessly. I think that she picked up about twenty-six mallard ducklings that one day and handled every one of them flawlessly. We worked her alone for that entire season and caught about sixteen hundred young mallards and around four hundred ducks of other species and Pat's mortality or accident rate was way less than one percent.

Harley and I were amazed at her performance. We watched her especially carefully one afternoon. We were working a beautiful pothole. It lay in a little valley and there were silver birch along the banks. This was up in the north bush country. We ran four broods of young ducks out of that pothole. It is the nature of the wild duck to leave the water and hide while you are still some distance away. The ducklings are small and they hide very completely in the tall grass.

Well, we lost Pat.

She was well trained to the whistle and I really sat down on that whistle, blowing it hard to bring her back.

But she just wouldn't respond. She wouldn't come in. After about ten minutes of blowing, I began to get sort of frantic. Something had happened to her. I was sure of that.

We had seen some ducks go into this aspen thicket nearby and so I went in there and looked and looked. Ducks were running everywhere. All this time, I was frantically blowing Pat in on the whistle, but no sign of her.

Finally I found her in a most peculiar position. I would have given anything for my camera! She had a pintail duck in her mouth. She caught the pintail and on her way back, she jumped a mallard that was almost fully grown. She had chased that mallard down and she was lying there with both front feet holding that mallard and with the pintail still in her mouth.

When she saw me she rolled those big eyes of hers and seemed quite relieved when I took both ducks from her.

There were always special little adventures around the "corner of the road" up there in Canada.

We were traveling down this country road one morning. It wasn't even gravel as most of them were, but just dirt. It had been graded up toward the center and after a little rain we'd had it was as slick as it could be.

Before Harley and I knew what had happened, the patrol car had slid off that damned road and gone down a thirty-foot bank. It didn't damage the car at all or didn't hurt us, but it was impossible to get the car back up that bank. There was just no way! It was still drizzling a little, but after a while the sun came out. Our only recourse was to simply sit there until that bank dried up enough for us to try to move the car.

We'd been sitting there for about an hour and a half. I had walked back up to the road. You could see to infinity both ways. Finally, as I was looking down this endless stretch of flat country road, I saw a dot and that dot grew bigger and bigger until it turned into a farm tractor.

I was delighted to see this farmer pull up beside me and stop his tractor. "You fellas havin' trouble?"

"Yes, sir, we slipped off this road bank during that little shower we just had and now we can't get the car out."

He scratched his head for a minute. "Well, I don't have a chain with me, but I have one down at the farm. I live about five miles down the road. I'll go get the chain and pull you out, but it'll take a little while."

I was afraid that might be the last we'd see of that ol' boy, but sure enough he finally came back with a chain and pulled us out. He even brought a larger tractor with him!

During the course of all this, we found out that his name was Lemange and we introduced ourselves. His nearest neighbor was six and a half miles from his place and he appeared to be starved for company.

"We're looking for potholes so we can count and band the ducks," we told him. This was a drought year up there and we were having a great deal of trouble finding ducks.

Well, he offered to take us around and show us the location of all the potholes that held water. I felt that we ought to pay him for the trouble we'd put him to.

"Mr. Lemange, we work for the United States government and

this car belongs to the U.S. The government pays for all of my expenses and I would certainly like to pay you for your trouble in pulling our car back on the road and for showing us the country."

He took it as an insult. "Don't ever try to pay a Canadian for helping a person out."

"I'm very sorry," I replied, "but back where I live, I'd have to pay a fellow fifty dollars before he'd ever hook the chain to the damned car!"

This Canadian farmer became one of our best friends up there. "I want you to follow me on up to the house. I told my wife and she is preparing some lunch."

So we went on behind the tractor, down that Canadian dirt road to the farmhouse. It was immaculate. The place was beautiful. It was on the prairie, but it had trees planted on three sides of it for windbreaks.

We went on in and met his lovely wife. She not only had a snack for us, but a bountiful meal and we must have sat at that table for an hour or so just talking and eating.

That afternoon, this Canadian wheat farmer took us all over the country and showed us all of the potholes that held water that year and where the ducks were nesting. Then he brought us back to his home and that evening we had dinner with him, had some of the best antelope steak that I have ever tasted. He turned out to be quite a hunter. He hunted in the lower part of Saskatchewan Province down near the Montana line and that is really good antelope country.

After dinner, he told us about another farm some fifteen miles up the road. "There's some good water and plenty ducks up there," he said.

So, the next day, we drove into this farmyard and introduced ourselves.

"We're United States conservation officers. I'm Bill Parker and this is Harley Pierson and we're up here banding ducks for study purposes. We met your neighbor, Mr. Lemange, who lives a couple of sections over from here and he told us that you might have some water on your place that we could work."

This farm also had a very nice home on it. There was the farmer, his wife, and two young daughters, who were both obviously pregnant.

He insisted that we come in and have tea, although it was still early in the day. We found out that the grandmother of the family had just come over from England. She had a decided British accent. The farmer told us that there was a major pothole on the place right behind his house about a quarter of a mile and that we could go there and band ducks if we wanted to.

Well, Harley and I went on back there and we were astounded to find not a pothole, but actually a small lake of about five or six acres.

Young ducks, which are still unable to fly, just won't leave a body of water like that. They just get right in the middle of it and group up, but we had a solution to this problem of how to catch these damn ducks.

We kept a little Manitoba trap, a set trap that has wings on it you can snap shut, in the car. Well, we got that out and set it up on the lake and Harley and I were preparing to drive the ducks into it, but we had our doubts. There was a lot of water for only two men to cover, herding half-grown ducks.

We heard a noise behind us and looked around. Here was the farmer and his wife and his two pregnant daughters in a line coming across that lake to help us out. They were almost up to their necks, wading through that stagnant water.

With their help, we drove most of those ducks into the trap and there was Grandmother on the bank cheering us on. "There goes one!" she'd yell in her thick British accent.

Before we were through, we had caught every duck on that lake. We had about 110 ducks that we carried to the bank and proceeded to sex and band.

When you sex a duck, you have to open the rectum so that you can see their sexual organs, which are recessed. You look for a penis, which on a young duck resembles a small white worm. If it's got a penis then the duck is, of course, a male. If you don't see a penis, then you can be sure the duck is female. It's as simple as that. The penis is rather obvious even on a young duck, and you can find it without any trouble.

I knew damned well that as soon as we started this operation, we would have to explain this procedure to the entire family, including Grandma, and I just didn't want to get involved with that subject, which could have got as hairy as a bear, talking sex with a Canadian family with a British background, all very proper and that sort of thing. So Harley and I decided that we would go right ahead and sex them, band them, age them, and take our notes, but we'd use a code system.

I was examining the ducks while Harley was keeping the notes. When I'd sex a male, I'd yell out, "That's a *B.*" If it was female, I'd say it was a *G.*

We had only sexed six or eight birds and Grandmother was a little hard of hearing. She leaned over to her daughter, the farm wife, and whispered, but it sounded like thunder. "What's he looking in them ducks' asses for?"

I like to have collapsed and Harley's face got red, but we kept right on working. Her daughter ignored the old woman.

So Grandmother leaned over again to her daughter and this time it was louder. "What's he looking in them ducks' asses for?" She was insistent on an answer.

I said, "My God, I can explain it to you. Many of these birds have internal parasites. We are just checking to see if they have worms." I showed her and she examined the duck closely as did the rest of the family.

"About half of them got worms?" observed this old British lady.

"That's right," I replied.

So we went right ahead and sexed and banded 126 ducks, all of us as muddy as we could be. Then we went back to the farmhouse and had tea.

chapter 17

Maryland, the Free State (For Some Hunters)

DURING THE WINTER of 1965–66, there were no surprises left for me in Kentucky. I knew what was around the bend of every stream, the turn of every road. Through the experience I had gained and my informers, I knew just about what would happen; I knew where it would happen, and when it would happen.

In a sense, it was almost like watching a movie for the second time. I began to get restless.

Then in May of 1966, an event occurred that electrified all of the agents that were in the area, including me. Washington announced that the Fish and Wildlife Service of the Department of the Interior intended to replace the wildlife agent in charge of the state of Maryland.

This announcement made one of the top supervisory positions in the eastern region open. I wanted that position and my wife, Faye, encouraged me to try for it.

I had about nine years of service with the Fish and Wildlife Service at this time. I had worked hard, so I had no reason to believe that I would not be seriously considered for this choice position.

The position was finally advertised through the channels. I made application for it and I was accepted!

Well, after I knew that I was to get the job, my kids, Ronnie, 12, and Rita, 17, ran to the public library in Henderson, Kentucky, our hometown, and got some maps of Maryland. I had never been to the state in my life, so we all took a look.

"Why, it's a tiny state!" I said to the kids. "Compare Maryland with the state of Pennsylvania. Compare it to the state of Kentucky, Tennessee, or Louisiana, and you can see that it's very small.

"That new job will be no problem. I can easily take care of a small state like that!"

I flew to Baltimore on May 29, 1966, to look things over and got into what was then Friendship International Airport at about ten in the morning. I was met there by Federal Game Warden Larry Thurman, a dedicated and generally quiet sort of man. Thurman was also a pilot for the Fish and Wildlife Service and he came to meet me in a Super Cub aircraft that I was to get to know very well over the next few years.

We flew from the Baltimore airport (Larry had parked the Cub on the grass next to the commercial runway), and this was all strange country to me then, but country that I now know so well.

They call Maryland "America in Miniature" and that is exactly what it is. Its mountainous regions lie to the west of the state; its beautiful Piedmont area of gently rolling farmland is in the center and to the north. Maryland's coastal plain, where the state was "born" with its first settlement along the beautiful St. Mary's River in southern Maryland, lies to both the south and the east and borders the great and beautiful Chesapeake Bay. The miles of shoreline of the Chesapeake is broken by countless rivers and thousands of acres of saltwater marsh.

It is this area that is of prime interest to hundreds of thousands of waterfowl: wild duck of many species, immense flocks of wild Canadian geese—flocks so large that they can cover an entire field like a "chicken yard"—and even flocks of the huge white wild swan—great, snow-white birds that were nearly extinct not too many years ago.

This Chesapeake Bay area, of interest to the migrating waterfowl each autumn, was of course of great interest to a large number of hunters of all descriptions, ranging from real sportsmen to market hunters. It was therefore of prime interest to me as well.

So Larry Thurman and I flew from Baltimore's airport, southwest of the city, heading just a little south of the mouth of the Patapsco

River, around Gibson Island at mid-bay, and then flew down the bay itself and across some four miles of its blue-green waters southeast of Baltimore, finally arriving at Easton midway on the Eastern Shore.

On this initial trip, I saw what I then thought was a considerable area of the Chesapeake Bay. There were duck blinds everywhere. I saw extensive marshes, many, many of those creeks and rivers that give the Chesapeake its jagged shoreline and its special attraction to the waterfowl.

Of course, as this was early spring, there were no migrating waterfowl. These great V-flights of the Canada geese and swan and the flights of ducks were to begin arriving here in late September and the flights from the far north would continue throughout November.

After we set down at the Easton airport, Agent Thurman and I drove to Cambridge some miles below and across the Choptank River to the U.S. Fish and Wildlife Service office that was located there.

On that introductory trip, I spent five days on Maryland's Eastern Shore as I was taking charge of the U.S. Fish and Wildlife operation and property in the state. I was trying to see as much as I could in a short time, trying to evaluate the situation and make some intelligent plans by meeting and talking to the federal personnel who were stationed in Maryland at the time.

One of my major stops was a visit to the huge Blackwater National Wildlife Refuge below Cambridge, a fascinating place that harbored wildlife of all descriptions, including bald eagles, waterfowl, and the nearly extinct Bryant fox squirrel, a large gray squirrel that is now found in only five Eastern Shore counties of Maryland.

After I had been down on the Shore for a few days, we had a beautiful, windless clear day, so I got Larry Thurman to fly me over all of the bay waters of the state.

We must have put in at least seven hours of flying. We looked at the large expanse of Dorchester County marshes, on down into

Somerset County, then swung into Worcester County and looked at the Atlantic Ocean.

I was greatly impressed by the "vastness" of what was really a comparably small area from what I had been used to. There were blinds on practically every marsh pond, everywhere you looked. If the waterfowling stories that I had heard were true, the stories of expansive baiting of waterfowl and of market hunters, then I had really got myself a job!

It was apparent that there was nothing I had done in my entire career as a state and federal game warden that could compare with the job I was undertaking. I really had no idea at the time just exactly the scope of the assignment I was taking on.

My family and I left Henderson, Kentucky, on the last day of June and arrived in Annapolis, the capital of Maryland, on the Fourth of July. It was an extremely hot day and far from "Independence Day" as far as my personal life was concerned.

For the next eight years, my entire life was to be devoted to the enforcement of the Migratory Bird Laws and to the protection and conservation of Maryland wildlife. That "hot" July day was indicative of what my life was to be while I was in the "Free State." I was really going to have to "sweat" to clear up some very bad situations!

Shortly after arriving at Annapolis, the first thing that I did was to move the federal Fish and Wildlife Service office from Cambridge up to the state capital where it was in a more central location and convenient to the center of state government and to the federal courts in Baltimore.

I then tried to determine just what my problems would be and what I was up against. I soon made an official visit to see George Shields, the director of the Maryland Game and Inland Fish Commission and this visit was extremely revealing.

Shields was unusually brief and outspoken. His point of view was clear and bluntly put. He told me, in no uncertain terms, that he was not under the orders or at the service of the federal game program man in Maryland. He looked me over as if to say, "Well, I expect that you are just an extension of what we've had up here for years on the federal level and you can damn well go your own way just as long as you keep out of mine."

It wasn't until early September of my first year, 1966, in Maryland, when the dove season opened on September 6, that Shields began to permit his state wardens to work with us, to some extent.

My father-in-law had died just prior to the Maryland dove season opening and I had to return to Tennessee for his funeral. I left Tennessee on the night of September 5 and drove all night long and into the next morning to get back to Maryland for the opening, which was set for twelve noon.

I arrived at Annapolis at eleven-thirty. This just permitted me time to take a shower and get on some fresh clothes and meet the other federal game wardens that had been assembled at Annapolis.

At noon, just when the opening shots were fired, we began our work. There was one situation just outside of Annapolis in Anne Arundel County that had puzzled the federal agents as well as the Maryland Game and Inland Fish Commission for many years.

A man by the name of Carl Abend ran a commercial dove-shooting operation and I had been keeping my eye on him prior to the opening of the season throughout the latter part of August of that, my first year in Maryland. I found a considerable amount of wheat in some of his fields. So we hit Abend's place early in the afternoon on that opening day in September and I had never seen anything like it in my life.

Four of us hit the field that appeared to be heavily baited. There were about 150 hunters on that field or around its edges and the bait was still present.

You never saw such damn running! Men taking off in all directions! They were running through multiflora fences, running through the woods, across fields, automobiles were leaving in one hell of a hurry. It was a case of total confusion!

We managed to pick up fifty-six hunters and charged them with shooting over bait. We picked up Abend, the owner, and we charged him with aiding and abetting in the violation of the Federal Game and Migratory Bird Laws.

This was the first of many significant cases that were to drastically change the hunting habits of a good number of Maryland "sportsmen."

Later, during that same month of September and during the same year, I worked my first clapper rail season. A clapper rail is a long-legged aquatic bird, a marsh bird. The successful method of hunting this bird involves waiting for high tide. This isolates the clapper rail on clumps of marsh grass. The hunters then paddle or row their boats within range and when the bird flushes, they shoot it.

Much of the clapper rail hunting took place in tidewater Virginia, in Accomack County, which is a peninsula extending down from Maryland's Eastern Shore with the Chesapeake Bay on one side and the Atlantic Ocean on the other. The shoreline of this island is perfect railbird habitat, being mostly saltwater marsh and countless small islands. The people here have been here for generations and have the same general attitude about game laws that their ancestors must have had.

At any rate, there was a good deal of illegal shooting of clapper rail in the area with the use of a motor-powered boat rather than oars. Limits didn't mean much in this area either and just about the only limitation on the number of birds a hunter took depended upon how many he was able to shoot!

We decided to change all that. Up to this point, the regulations had seldom been enforced and these people were having themselves a ball.

I pulled all of the federal wildlife officers out of Maryland for a special raid on the clapper railbird shooters of Accomack County.

Larry Thurman took the Super Cub down there and flew at about twenty-five hundred feet, working as a spotter. You could hardly see the plane.

We had four boats in the area getting reports from a spotter flying with Larry. From up there, you could see the prop wash, the wake from an outboard motor on a boat, and since the clapper rail are low-flying birds, the men in the plane could actually see the birds flush. They could see the shot pattern as the gunshot hit the water and they could see where the bird fell, and since the clapper is also a slow-flying bird, most of them were killed.

Well, one afternoon on a high tide down there, the observer in the plane called me and said, "There's a white boat over by the old Coast Guard station. I watched him kill eight rail with his motor running. There are two men in the boat."

Well, this was a good two miles away, but I started over there at high speed and, of course, they saw me coming. By the time I got there, they had the motor shut off and propped up out of the water and were using a couple of poles, pushing the boat through the marshy area.

I pulled alongside. "I'm a federal game warden and I want to have a look at your hunting licenses."

I counted the birds and checked them out, then I said, "Gentlemen, I will have to take some information from you and issue you a summons. You've been shooting clapper rail from this boat with the use of a motor and that's a violation of the federal regulations."

One of them answered, "Well, Mr. Warden, just how could you tell that we had the damn motor running? We saw you coming when you were a mile and a half away and you couldn't see what we were doing from that distance."

"That's right," I replied.

"Well, then, just how in the hell could you tell that we were shooting rail with the motor running?" These two fellows were pretty sure that they had me.

I just pointed my finger up to the sky.

"That man up there told me," I replied.

Well, the most astonished look came over the faces of both of those hunters. One of them shook his head in bewilderment.

"Well, hell, if you've got *Him* deputized, I guess that we might just as well quit hunting!"

We made an awful lot of rail bird cases down there in Tidewater, Virginia, that year but were not very well received in the United

States District Court at Norfolk, although this section of Tidewater, Virginia, was within my jurisdiction. It was apparent that the United States attorney's office for the eastern section of Virginia was not going to prosecute very many of our cases. We understood their position. After all, these were petty offenses and misdemeanors and they had better things to do. These cases were, however, very important to the protection of our wildlife resources and it took a while to convince the United States attorney and the courts in both Virginia and Maryland to recognize this fact.

This was one of my major problems in the new job.

chapter 18

The Awakening of the Judicial System

DURING MY FIRST year in Maryland, we were not able to prosecute any cases in the federal court system. The United States District Court in Baltimore was absolutely overloaded. They had one hell of a backlog that related to important felonies. In fact, we didn't prosecute a single case in the federal courts until we began to break the judicial ice a little during the following year: the season of 1967–68.

During that first waterfowl season that I was in Maryland, the fall and winter of 1966–67, we had arrested some nine hundred of those Maryland "sportsmen," mostly for illegal baiting of waterfowl and over-limit violations. These people we caught were amazed at this drastic change in the situation because before this they were, in many areas of the Chesapeake Bay country, left pretty much undisturbed. But if they were amazed by our activity, they weren't worried.

Practically every one of these hunters we caught at one violation or another were quick to show us a receipt from a Maryland state court indicating that they had posted a fine and had paid collateral in the amount of $26.56 for a state charge of shooting over bait, and they were proud of this. They weren't at all hesitant to tell you, "Why, certainly, I'm a member of the "Twenty-six-Fifty-six Club! In fact, I have a double membership, I've been caught twice!"

This small amount of money meant nothing to these Eastern Shore waterfowlers who were divided into two major groups. One group consisted of the very wealthy sportsmen and large property owners on the Chesapeake Bay. Many of these people had come here to retire and many of them were millionaires.

The other group of Eastern Shore gunners that I encountered through my work in Maryland was made up of the people whose families had lived for generations on the bay, its rivers, and marshes. And like the Louisiana backcountry Cajuns, these people of the "Maryland marshes" had little respect for any game laws whatsoever. A lot of these watermen-hunters were not poor by any means and many a sportsman carried along as "legal ammunition" a big bank roll besides his shotgun shells and other equipment.

During the season of 1966, if one man showed me a neatly folded one-hundred-dollar bill tucked in the plastic holder along with his hunting license, then five hundred hunters must have shown me the same thing!

They would laugh and say, "This is my hunting license! I figure that anything I do or anything I get caught at, that one-hundred-dollar bill will take care of it!"

This really astounded me; for the first time in my life I was dealing with a section of the hunting public that not only had little respect for the laws, but who didn't seem to have any concern over money either.

By the way things were going in Maryland, I could predict that unless some major steps were taken in the courts to deter these people, much of the waterfowl in the Atlantic flyway was in jeopardy.

Throughout the entire waterfowl season of 1966, we did nothing but run from blind to blind, checking as many hunters as we possibly could, issuing as many summonses as was possible in a day, every day of the week, and simply filing the information we took in files, waiting for a time when the season closed and things slowed down a little.

Then we would have to decide what we were going to do with all of these damned cases. Hopefully, we would get at least some of them into the federal courts.

During the spring of 1967, the Baltimore press and a couple of the Washington, D.C., papers launched a bitter attack against the federal game wardens in Maryland, including myself, as a result of our intensified law enforcement activity.

I tried my damndest to get a lawyer to make a libel suit against one particular reporter who was especially vicious in his reporting but, since he didn't mention names, there was no way we could fight back. We were upsetting the "sportsmen's" applecart and reaping a lot of resentment as a result.

These attacks continued through the summer of 1967 but then, in the autumn of that year, just before the dove season opened, we began to get some very favorable publicity from the Baltimore *Evening Sun* newspaper. Bill Burton, outdoor writer for this paper, had always supported conservation of our wildlife as well as our federal program of wildlife law enforcement in its entirety. He has consistently made an outstanding effort and contribution to the cause.

Just before things began to get busy in 1967, we got that break in the federal court system that I had been waiting for. We had a change in United States attorneys with the coming of a brilliant young attorney, Theodore McKeldin, Jr., to the United States attorney's office in Baltimore.

Young McKeldin was assigned to the bird cases, the violations of the Migratory Bird Treaty Act. Somehow, during the turmoil of World War I, the United States and Canada had found the time to consider the plight—and the wholesale destruction—of migratory birds, especially wild waterfowl. Thus, the Migratory Bird Treaty Act came into being and was implemented by law in 1918, providing for the protection of migratory birds and for controls over the hunting and shooting of them. It was not until 1937 that a third nation, Mexico, signed a similar treaty with the United States. Now, most major countries participate in the protection of migratory birds under the act.

Well, I knew that McKeldin's father was the former governor of Maryland, the former mayor of Baltimore, and had been a prominent political figure in Maryland for many years. And so, naturally, I expected Ted, Jr., to be deeply influenced by the political aspects of the cases that I was trying to make.

But on my first meeting with Ted, I was delighted and surprised to discover an intelligent and personable young lawyer who was well versed in the out-of-doors. He was a hunter. He understood precisely the language that I was talking and what I was trying to do.

There was one time, however, when that "language" got a little screwed up.

I had smoked cigarettes just about all my life, starting the habit at a very young age but, while I was working in Maryland during 1969, I decided that I would quit smoking. I thought that I was a very strong person and that I could control myself under any circumstance. I did quit smoking for a period of twenty-one days.

Then I found out just how addicted I was to the habit. During this interval, to relieve the extreme nervous tension that built up in me, I began to chew tobacco as an alternative. I was never very good at this country pastime, but I was careful because I knew that "chaw tobacco" was kind of potent, especially if you swallowed accidentally and some of the juice got into your digestive system.

I went to Baltimore one day on a very important assignment. I was to appear before a federal grand jury to indict some individuals in some very serious migratory bird cases.

The procedure involved the twenty-six men and women on the grand jury, an assistant United States attorney, and me; we would be the only ones in the room.

I would testify before the grand jury, giving them a narrative statement of the facts relating to the cases, then I would retire, and sometime later the grand jury would either render a "True Bill" or a "No True Bill."

Well, I got up there that morning and young Ted McKeldin was the assistant United States attorney representing us at that time. I had a pouch of Beechnut chewing tobacco stuck in my pocket and I asked, "Ted, how long will we be before that grand jury?"

"Only three or four minutes," he answered.

Well, appearing before a grand jury or any jury for that matter, I have always been awed and impressed by the federal judicial system. Certainly, I wanted to make a good appearance before this grand jury and I was just a little bit nervous, not because of appearing before a grand jury but simply because I had been off of cigarettes.

I decided that I would risk putting a generous portion of this Beechnut chewing tobacco tucked away back in my mouth and that would relieve my anxiety.

We walked down that long hall, Ted and I, and went in that federal grand jury room and I was expecting to stay about three or four minutes.

I sat there at the table with Assistant United States Attorney McKeldin and, in this grand jury room, they had a speaker's podium and when you addressed the grand jury, you stood behind that.

McKeldin introduced me to the grand jury. "Agent Parker has a statement to make to the grand jury," and he turned me over to them. I got up behind that podium. I made my little spiel, giving them the basic, essential facts of these cases which were all related, involving three people.

This jury was impressed by the fact that the federal government was interested in the protection of birds. They began to ask questions. The three minutes stretched to six minutes and this chew of tobacco was getting bigger by the minute! It was becoming almost impossible for me to articulate, at least to sound intelligent, because my mouth was full of tobacco juice.

It soon became painfully apparent to me that there was no relief from this situation, no escape and nowhere for me to go. I did the only thing that was left to do: I swallowed the whole cud of tobacco!

That tobacco hit my stomach like a stick of dynamite and I immediately became violently nauseated and, yet, I couldn't admit that I was ill.

I'm before a federal grand jury and I'm a professional law enforcement officer. There was nothing I could do but stand there. I began to feel myself getting pale. I was dizzy and I felt a cold sweat beading on my upper lip and forehead.

I stood there before that grand jury for thirty minutes and answered innumerable questions from every one of those twenty-six jurists, just barely able to stay conscious and barely able to make my answers intelligible.

When I walked out of the grand jury room, Ted McKeldin, Jr., had noticed my obvious discomfort and he had noticed the fact that I had gone completely pallid and he could see the sweat on my forehead.

"Bill," he said, as we walked down that long hall that was beginning to sway like some sort of damned snake, "Bill, I don't think I've ever seen a grand jury get to you like that one did!"

"What do you mean?"

"You'd been up there about ten minutes. Suddenly you got very pale and your voice began to quiver a little bit and——"

"Ted, I had just swallowed an ounce and a half of chewing tobacco!"

"Oh, my God, Bill! No wonder you're ill!"

I went back to smoking cigarettes.

We had seventy-two cases pending when Ted McKeldin took over our business there in the United States attorney's office in Baltimore. He immediately filed those seventy-two cases, many of which we won. For the first time, the hunting public was beginning to sit up and take notice.

Ted left that office sometime the following year and was replaced by another brilliant young man but, unlike Ted McKeldin, Fred Motz had led a rather sheltered city life and knew next to nothing about hunting, or the hunting laws that I was trying to enforce.

I will never forget my first meeting with this young man. I went to his office to talk with him.

"I'm Bill Parker, federal wildlife officer in charge of the Maryland District, Mr. Motz, and I would like to talk to you about some of the cases we have pending."

"Fine," he said. "I have the time."

"I want to talk to you about a man who has killed seven American widgeon and . . ."

"What is an American widgeon?" the young United States attorney asked.

I thought, hmmmm! "Well, Mr. Motz, possibly you know it by its colloquial name. It's a baldpate."

"What's a baldpate?"

"Mr. Motz, a baldpate is a wild duck. It's a migratory waterfowl."

"Oh!" he replied. "I see."

I asked him, "May I inquire about your background, please? Have you ever hunted?"

"No."

"Have you ever fished?"

"No."

"Have you ever used a weapon?"

"No, I have never fired a gun in my life. I was reared in Baltimore City. I do like to water ski though."

Now here was a United States attorney who I had to work with on important cases who knew absolutely nothing about wildlife or my work. He was totally different from young Ted McKeldin. But he was very enthusiastic about being a member of the United States attorney's office.

So he and I began a long period of training. It was a mutually beneficial situation. Fred Motz taught me law and I taught him about wildlife and conservation.

In less than three months, Fred Motz was standing up before the court quite comfortable with terms like "redhead" and "canvasback"; night shooting, baiting, and all of the problems connected with my job and the cases he was prosecuting, and the crimes that were being committed against the migratory waterfowl and wildlife of the Chesapeake Bay area.

Motz was well versed in the law and when he became knowledgable about the things that we as federal wildlife officers do, he became a most competent assistant United States attorney.

Now, because of his lack of knowledge in this highly specialized field, I told him: "Anytime we're in the United States District Courts [prior to the forming of the United States Magistrates' Courts in 1969], when I feel that you're going astray in your presentation to the court, or that you are getting in 'muddy waters' or a place where you shouldn't be in your statement, I'll tug on your coattail. And when I tug on your coattail, I expect you to stop the things you're saying and get off on a different course." I was motivated simply by wanting this brilliant young man to be aware of certain things that I had learned from painful experience.

There was a time during a jury trial on a baiting case just before his final address to the jury that I felt that he was getting into a dangerous area concerning how much corn constituted baiting. I tugged on his coattail a couple of times and got no response. Fred Motz, the assistant United States attorney, continued on his merry way. I knew that it was disconcerting as hell to be interrupted because an attorney has to concentrate totally on what he is doing and saying. In winding up a case, he is down to the "nut-cutting" and what he says in summation requires total concentration.

After I had tugged on his coattail a couple of times to get him off this dangerous subject and got no response from him whatsoever, I tapped him on his left shin with my foot. He was standing at the same table where I was sitting.

I was the government's chief prosecuting witness. Motz was a tall, thin young man and when I tapped him on the shin, he immediately asked the court's indulgence and leaned way down to reach my ear.

"What's the trouble?" he whispered.

"Thank God you stopped that tack. Here is the danger you are about to get involved in. I want you to please consider this danger before you proceed."

He said, "Thank you very much, I can see the problem with that course now."

He went back to his summation of the case and expertly blended what he had said with what he was about to say. We eventually got through that case to our satisfaction, and I learned that day that the best way to get a lawyer's attention, without being held in contempt if the judge sees you, is to simply kick him in the shins under the defense table where the judge can't see what's going on.

If you hit that attorney with a hard-toe shoe, you will definitely get his attention.

Well, Mr. Motz represented us for a long period of time and his record was fantastic. I don't believe that we lost a case while he was our prosecutor.

But all good things have both a beginning and an end. The United States attorney's office in Baltimore was a sort of training ground for young attorneys. Some brilliant young lawyers have gone through that office.

The office by this time was headed by George Beall and when Fred Motz left, I was quite a bit worried about who would replace him in prosecuting our cases. He had reached the place where, you might say, because of painful experience, he was getting very skillful before the court in prosecuting our waterfowl cases.

Mr. Beall was considerate enough to let me make some suggestions and I recommended Michael E. Marr, a member of the staff. Although he was relatively new in the United States attorney's office at the time, I had met Mr. Marr and was impressed by both his manner and his intelligence. He had the makings of a very fine lawyer.

Mike was about six feet, weighed 185 pounds, wore one hell of a moustache. He was a very personable, dynamic young man.

Well, Mr. Marr was assigned to the cases that originated in my Maryland federal fish and wildlife district. Although Mr. Marr was a brilliant young man, he was also very headstrong. He, like Fred Motz, had no experience relating to the out-of-doors, to hunting and, specifically, to waterfowl.

By this time, in 1969, we had the United States Magistrates' Courts system, which gave us, for the first time, the opportunity to try an unlimited number of misdemeanor cases, a factor in breaking the back of illegal waterfowl hunting in Maryland. Prior to this, only a token number of such cases ever went to court, not more than fifty.

Mr. Marr was spending as much as four days a week prosecuting violations of the Migratory Bird Treaty Act. He had remarkable self-confidence and once he got on his feet on the floor, I saw that he believed that he could handle any situation that came down the pike!

I shared his confidence—up to a point. However, I had been sitting beside United States attorneys on cases of the type that we had in Maryland, and I had been burned badly many times by very simple and insignificant things in the course of a trial.

It was quite easy for me to offer this young man advice as to what he should stay away from and how he should proceed. But as we progressed, he completely ignored my suggestions and the fact that I had made the same deal with him that I had made with Fred Motz. I would tug on his coat if I thought he was getting into dangerous waters.

"Mr. Marr," I told him, "if I don't get your attention the first time I tug on your coat, I am going to put a damn good jerking on that coattail of yours and, then, if I still don't get your attention, I am going to take what I deem appropriate action."

"That will be fine," he said, but he thought that he could handle all that jazz that came through the federal court.

Well, Mr. Michael Marr was addressing the United States Magistrates' Court in Baltimore one day and he began to stray from the subject at hand and get into a field that I thought was dangerous because, if he explored it, that would open it up for the defense attorney to go the same route. I thought that this might be damaging to our case, so I tugged on his coat. He proceeded merrily on his way, paying no attention at all to me.

I was doing this under the table where the judge couldn't see me. I reached up a little farther and jerked the hell out of his coat. Mike frowned but proceeded with the mistake he was making.

Well, I turned sideways in my chair, looked at him intently as I kicked with my left foot on his left shin. I kicked him as hard as I could.

He was a young man of considerable composure! A pained expression came over his face. "A moment's indulgence, Your Honor. May I confer with Agent Parker?"

The judge nodded his approval. "Go ahead."

Marr leaned down and whispered to me, as if he were asking me a vital question. "You son of a bitch, if you ever kick me under that damned table again, I'm going to break your neck!" He said all this without so much as changing his professional courtroom demeanor the slightest bit.

"I am distressed that I had to use that method to get your attention, Mr. Marr, but the direction you are taking in this case is extremely dangerous and please leave that alone and return to the orderly business of prosecuting this case."

"I'll take care of you out in the hall," he whispered back, and I replied, "Yes, and I'll take care of *you* out in the hall! If you lose this case for me, it's going to be your ass!"

He immediately stood up and resumed but, like his predecessor, Mr. Motz, he was so well trained and so professional that he was able to blend what he was about to say with what he had already said. The interruption and the change in direction was not too noticeable to either the court or to the defense attorney.

We won the case.

Afterward, out in the hall, Mr. Marr came up to me and said, "Let me tell you. My shin is tender and you have badly bruised it. You quit knocking me under that damned table!"

"I'll quick kicking you under that table as long as you permit me to get your attention by a simple jerk on your coat."

Some weeks later, we were involved in another case concerning the baiting of geese that was of paramount importance. Mr. Marr again launched into an area that I considered dangerous. Marr began so eloquently to refer to an irrelevant case, and I tugged his coattail. He was so intent on what he was doing that he ignored this. So I put out a damn good jerking on his coattail. He completely ignored me again. I again turned in my chair and kicked the hell out of his left shin, which by this time must have been getting pretty damned tender.

The same pained expression came over his face and we went through the same procedure that we had been through before.

About a week or two after the fifth time I had to rake Mike across his shins, one of the United States magistrates called me into his chambers and asked me, "Is Mr. Marr handling all of your cases?"

"Yes, sir, he is."

"Well, does he have a physical impairment?"

"Judge, I am not aware of any physical impairment on his part. Why do you ask me that?"

"Well," the magistrate replied, "I've noticed five or six times in the last month that he will suddenly get a very pained expression on his face, right in the middle of something that he is saying to the court. In every instance he will say, 'A moment's indulgence, Your Honor! May I confer with Agent Parker?' After he confers with you, he appears to be relieved and stands up to proceed, but I've noticed that he changes direction."

I replied, "Actually, Judge, Mr. Marr has a very tender left shin and since he stands on his feet all day in prosecuting these matters for us, I imagine that he gets very tired. When you see that pained expression on his face, it is probably due to the fact that he has some minor pain that is associated with his tender left shin." Of course, I never told the judge what really went on under the table.

During one of my earlier conversations with Michael Marr, I asked him, "How would you feel about recommending to the court that they put some persons in jail, persons who have committed a very aggravated offense or someone who is a repeated violator of our Wildlife and Migratory Bird Laws?"

"Well," Mike said, "I would have no problem with that. In fact, I think that the type of person you have described belongs in jail. Bring me one and I'll show you that I will have no hesitation in recommending to the court that they put him in jail for whatever term the law provides."

Well, I walked out of that United States attorney's office in Baltimore on air that day. This is what I had been waiting for ever since I came to Maryland and saw how serious the situation was.

"I've got me a man in the United States district attorney's office who's got the nerve to do the things that need to be done," I was happily thinking.

Well, about a week later, this was in late November of 1969, just when the waterfowling season was picking up tempo and guns were going off all over the Chesapeake Bay country. Ol' Dan Searcy, one of my federal agents down in southern Maryland, hit the one we had been looking for.

He and a state agent from Maryland, Bob Arnold, caught two people down there with twenty-five ducks, most of them canvasbacks. That was well over the limit and besides that offense, they were also shooting over bait.

When we went to court with Mike Marr all primed and set to put it to 'em, we found that the defendants had hired themselves a St. Mary's County lawyer. He told the court that he didn't have adequate time to prepare defense and that he would like to continue the case.

Well, the damned case was postponed for thirty days. The case was rescheduled for the twenty-third day of December, just two days before Christmas.

This is a very bad time to try a case, especially when you are attempting to put a man in jail. Everyone has a benevolent attitude at that time of year, including a United States magistrate! During the Christmas season, they begin to feel charitable toward these people who come before them.

Mike Marr prosecuted this case. I believe that it was his first case involving the Migratory Bird Treaty Act, or at least one of his first cases of this nature.

It was one hell of a trial. We began at nine o'clock in the morning and there were several motions, including one to suppress the evidence that we had collected.

By eleven-thirty, all of the evidence was in and Judge Daniel Kline issued his ruling. He found both defendants guilty on all charges. I was sure that he would because the evidence we had was overwhelming.

After the ruling, I punched Mike Marr. "OK, bud, right now is the time. Let's recommend that there be no fine, no probation, just ninety days in jail. You really got to come on strong, Mike. We've got to have this!"

Well, Mike was loquacious as hell. He took to his feet and he said, "Your Honor, for many years this type of case has been prosecuted in the federal court system in this district and for all of those years, the United States attorney's office has recommended nominal penalties and a few rather heavy fines in some cases. It is apparent to the federal wildlife agents that we have not established the desired level of deterrent that is absolutely necessary if we are to protect these birds the way they must be protected."

Mr. Marr continued. "Your Honor, this case involves the canvasback duck. The principal species the defendants killed illegally were canvasbacks. The canvasback does not yet appear on the endangered species list, but I am certain and so are the federal wildlife agents that the canvasback duck is already in a threatened or endangered status.

"Now these two men wantonly and with complete disregard for their actions baited this creek and killed canvasback in substantial numbers. This type of conduct in the hunting element of the public must be deterred. The canvasback is on the brink of extinction!

"Now because of all these things that I have listed for the court, the United States attorney's office is not interested in merely the payment of a fine. We are interested in punitive action that will serve as a deterrent for the future conduct of these two people who have been convicted in this court and their neighbors as well.

"Now by virtue of all of these reasons and for the first time in Maryland, the United States attorney's office comes before this court and recommends that Your Honor assess no fine against these defendants, that you assess no probation against these defendants, that you sentence each of these men to ninety days in jail!"

There was a stunned silence in that courtroom. There was the United States attorney's office standing up in open court and requesting that waterfowl hunters be sentenced to prison for killing wild ducks!

These two men had a pretty damned good lawyer. In rebuttal, he got up and said, "Your Honor, down there in St. Mary's County there is a little home that sets in a small valley. It is not a pretentious home. It is of frame construction and it is rather small. In the corner of this home," the lawyer continued, "there is a Christmas tree. It is not the expensive kind, the artificial tree that most people buy, but it is a scraggly pine that was cut off a hillside down there. And, Your Honor, that tree is not decorated with all of the expensive balls and tinsel that most people know. It is simply decorated with strings of popcorn, pinecones, and things that the kids collected themselves.

"Now there is no fireplace in this home, Your Honor, but there is a stove and a mantel and from this mantel there hang four little stockings in anticipation of Santa Claus, the Man of Happiness, coming to this house tomorrow evening. Both of my clients are in the same position, Your Honor, and I don't believe that you can find it in your heart at this time to take these men away from their families two days before Christmas just for killing ducks."

Well, I knew that we had a problem. It *was* the Christmas season that was upon us.

The defense lawyer sat down. The United States attorney has the last lick in these matters.

Mike got up and he said, "Your Honor, it might be bad to take these men away from their families over Christmas, but the government has a solution for that problem. We recommend that you sentence the defendants to ninety days in prison, but allow them to begin their sentences on January the tenth. That will give them ample time to enjoy the Christmas and the New Year's holidays."

By this time, it was approaching twelve noon. About two minutes to twelve, all statements had been made, including that of the United States attorney, Mike Marr.

The judge was considering all that had been said and finally he made this statement:

"I find the recommendation of the government to be reasonable. It is absolutely essential that the court establish a deterrent to the conduct of people who insist upon shooting waterfowl in violation of the federal laws."

I leaned back in my chair. It had been a damned tense time, but now I thought that we had it made!

The courtroom was as silent as Death itself. It was a crowded courtroom waiting for the sentence.

And at that precise instant, just as the judge was about to speak, there came the pealing of Christmas bells from a church near the Federal Building, a carillon playing that beautiful Christmas hymn, "Oh, Come All Ye Faithful." The music poured into that courtroom. . . . "Joyful and Triumphant!"

I punched Mike in the ribs and whispered, "Hump up, because here comes Santa Claus. We've had it!"

Well, the most peculiar look came over Judge Kline's face and he looked straight at me, sitting there at the prosecution table and he said, "It is the judgment of this court that each defendant pay a four-hundred-and-fifty-dollar fine, that he be placed on probation for a period of two years and, as a condition of that probation, he cannot hunt any bird protected by the federal government during the period of time of the probation."

Well, Mike and I walked out of that damned courtroom. I was absolutely stunned. A most unusual circumstance had prevented, at the last instant, something that was sure to happen: a jail sentence for offenders of the Migratory Waterbird Laws. It was bound to happen and it did, later, but the newspapers got hold of this particular case and worked it over. "CHRISTMAS CAROLS SAVE HUNTERS FROM JAIL."

chapter 19

The Informers

VERY EARLY DURING my tour of duty as agent in charge of the Maryland District of the United States Fish and Wildlife Service of the Department of the Interior, we found that there were a growing number of people who were dedicated to protecting wildlife, and especially the migratory waterfowl that came in huge flocks to the Free State.

The dedication of these people went far beyond the call of duty. They became a small army of informers who let us know whenever there was an illegal hunting activity going on and where to look for it.

Although "informer" is a distasteful word, the service of these people to our cause was immeasurable. Not only I, but all of the federal agents in Maryland, would get these calls and, as a result, we literally "tore up" the destructive, illegal hunters who preyed on the wildlife of Maryland's woods and waters.

This usually anonymous information was one factor that told me that our system of federal law enforcement pertaining to our wildlife resources in Maryland was beginning to work. We had excited a portion of the public who were interested in conservation and who did not like the slaughter that was going on against the waterfowl and mourning doves. These were the people who were "coming out of the woods" in increasing numbers.

One such case that I never will forget, and I can't mention the name because of harm that could still come to this informer, turned out to be one of the most important incidents that occurred during my years in Maryland.

I got the telephone call one night at my home around ten o'clock. The man on the phone had an extremely unusual voice that you could recognize anywhere.

I answered the ringing phone.

"I want to speak to Warden Parker."

"This is Parker. Can I help you?"

"Do you have something to write with?"

"Yes, I have." I always kept a yellow pad and a pencil right beside the phone for just such calls as this.

"All right. Listen carefully because I am not going to tell you this more than once. There's a certain farm on the northern section of the Eastern Shore [he named the area and the county] that lies on a certain creek.

"That farm is heavily baited. It's being baited about four or five times a week, and they are killing well in excess of the limit."

"Well," I asked, "can you give me any more information about it?"

"No," he answered, "I can't. I've told you all the information that I can give you."

I thanked him and said, "OK, I'll assure you that we'll look into this."

Well, I did look at this farm the next morning by airplane with Agent Larry Thurman. We saw an abnormal number of Canada geese, but we could see no bait or evidence of baiting except that one hell of a lot of geese were using this particular field.

Well, this was back in 1967 and we had a hell of a lot of farms there on the Eastern Shore to check out that year, so we weren't able to get back to check out this particular farm on a regular basis that season, and we did not apprehend anyone on that farm in 1967.

Some ten days before the waterfowl season in early October 1968, I received another telephone call; once again it came at ten o'clock at night.

I recognized that strange, unforgettable voice that said, "Well, you didn't touch that farm last year."

"No, I didn't. We didn't have the time."

"All right, listen close. I want to tell you just exactly what's going on over there. They are baiting that farm nightly now. They put two hundred and fifty pounds of corn out each night, in a silage field that runs down to the creek. The geese clean up the bait way ahead of the time you are able to get your plane out of Cambridge and fly over this place.

"They are already killing geese and there will be one hell of a kill on opening day.

"Now the method of baiting is this. They'll drive a pickup truck out of a shed about ten-thirty or eleven o'clock every night with just their parking lights on. They'll begin at the creek and spread this corn about two thirds of the way back up the hill. The corn is poured out of the back of the moving pickup."

My caller said in an urgent voice, "These people need to be caught. This needs to be stopped!"

"I can assure you that we will get right on this," I told him.

He gave me a hell of a lot more information than he realized. He let me know that he was extremely familiar with this place and the hunting operation that was going on there. He knew the method of baiting, he knew when, where, and how, and he knew the results.

It was certainly damned obvious to me that this caller had to be real close to the group that hunted this farm.

The next night, I drove over to this area of the northern Eastern Shore and hid my patrol car in a bunch of pine trees and then moved into a vantage point in a cornfield.

I got there in position about ten o'clock and just sat on the ground with my night glasses. It was a right pleasant night, late in October, some few days before the goose season opened.

Lo and behold, at ten thirty-five, I saw a light come on in the farm shed and I saw a pickup leave with just its parking lights on and it was heading in my direction. It came through a gate, drove on down to the creek, turned around, and drove slowly up through the cornfield, with only its parking lights still on.

The truck got about halfway to the top of the hill and stopped, maybe for three or four minutes, then started up again. With my glasses, I could determine that there were three people. One man was driving the truck and two people were in the back, shoveling corn.

He drove back to the shed and I stayed put, just sat there until all of the lights went out on this farm. Then I eased down to see what they had put out. Two golden streams of corn some 250 yards long, about a foot wide, and two or three inches deep.

I took some photographs and I took some samples and then I left.

The next night I had the same area staked out by one of my agents and at exactly ten-thirty, the operation was repeated.

We watched this damn baiting operation for five consecutive nights.

Two mornings I stayed over there in a place of concealment to see what the geese would do. Well, hell, just at daylight, they boiled out of that creek and they hit those two lines of corn and in less than twenty minutes, you couldn't have found a grain of corn in that field with a vacuum cleaner!

We set the place up for opening day and we set it up good. There were about eighteen blinds on that farm and on opening morning, the slaughter began.

I mean to tell you, they were really over-killing those damned geese. I've never seen wild geese come into any place like they came to that baited field.

When four of the blinds killed way over the limit, we decided to eliminate this illegal hunting, so we moved in.

And then the most peculiar thing happened. The first pit that we checked had four people in it.

"I'm Federal Game Agent Willie Parker," I told them. "I want you to get out of that pit. You are hunting in violation of the Migratory Waterbird Laws and I have to ask each of you several questions. What is your name? Age? Occupation? And height and weight?" I needed this information so that I could fill out my field violation reports.

It came as a tremendous surprise to discover that one man I checked in this pit was my confidential informer! I recognized his voice.

This really sent cold chills running up and down my back. Here was a man interested enough in conservation and in his sport to want to see a very destructive hunting practice stopped, and about the only way that he could see that it was stopped was to hunt it himself, or the other people would have known exactly who had been the informer. He knew that the evidence would come out at the trial that they had been reported by an anonymous caller.

This really floored me. I didn't change expression, didn't make any reference to anything, just took his information and handled him exactly the same way I handled the others.

I was completely professional and businesslike, but I had the strangest feeling when I walked off that damned field, and I said to myself as we walked away, "Hell, the things that I'm doing have got to be right. We'll have to win this war against the violators with men like that behind us!"

I came into Cambridge down midway on the Eastern Shore late one evening toward the end of 1968. Checked into the Quality Court Motel there just about nine o'clock.

There were maybe eighteen or twenty people standing around the bar in there and others sitting at the tables. The place was pretty well crowded.

I was seated at a table, and had just finished my sandwich and was drinking a glass of beer, when one of the fellows left the bar. He was wheeling a little bit and when he found his way indirectly to my table, he put his fingers to his lips and said, "Shhhh!"

I just looked at him. I didn't say anything and therefore there was no reason for me to "Shhhh."

He leaned over, still swaying, and I could smell the sour smell of booze on his breath.

"Let me tell you something," he said. "When the wind blows northwest and blows twenty-five knots, you go to John Tieder, Jr.'s place on Dark Road!"

I didn't pay much attention to this drunk.

Almost a year later, I was working some fifty or sixty miles north of Cambridge in Kent County. It was late November, but it was a warm, sunshiny day and I was working the goose fields, checking blinds and hunters.

I had on a wool shirt with the sleeves rolled up and it was hot! About eleven o'clock in the morning, the wind suddenly swung from the south to northwest. It increased in velocity and the next thing I knew, there was a full-fledged front coming through. Temperatures were dropping drastically and the wind got up to thirty, thirty-five knots.

It was getting toward the middle of the day and things are relatively quiet in the goose fields of Maryland about that time and I was wondering where I should go that afternoon. It was apparent that we were having a northwester and it was also apparent that the wild geese would move out.

While I was going into Chestertown, the county seat of Kent County, to get some lunch, I happened to remember the drunk and what he had said to me in that Cambridge bar nearly a year before.

"Well, hell! I'll go to Dorchester County and I'll just find John Tieder, Jr.'s place."

Bill Richardson lived at Cambridge in Dorchester County and worked the Blackwater National Wildlife Refuge southwest of Cambridge.

I contacted Larry Thurman and met him at Trappe, on the way to Cambridge. We went on to Bill Richardson's house and found him home.

"Bill, how about going out with us for a while?"

"OK, where are we going?"

"We're going to John Tieder, Jr.'s place. Where is it?"

"He's got two places."

"Which one does he hunt?"

Bill directed us to his farm. John Tieder, Jr., turned out to be a very prominent businessman who was well known in the Cambridge area. His farm was quite a place. We went in on an adjoining farm and pulled down a lane that ran along the Choptank River. Then we walked over to the edge of the woods where we could observe the Tieder farm.

We got in there about two P.M. or a little later, and it was cold and blowing. Those little scudding clouds were coming in across the Choptank. It was really a bad northwester!

We noted that there was a vehicle parked at the Tieder place, next to a barn. We also saw two geese come into a pit that was located out in the middle of a field nearby, and those two geese were promptly killed.

Three men got up out of that pit. One man took the two geese, carried them to a station wagon, and left.

That left two people in the pit and I mean to tell you that the damned geese really started flying. I saw some of the damndest shooting I have ever seen. The two men in that pit killed thirteen Canada geese without missing a shot. This put them well over the limit. The limit at that time was three per hunter.

It was getting rather late by now. I told Larry Thurman, "You go around and see if you can get on the other side of that pit, because they will be able to see us coming and we're probably going to have to chase them down, anyway. There's an excellent possibility that they can get away."

We had to cross quite a stretch of open field before we were able to reach the goose pit from where they were shooting.

We didn't have those little portable two-way radios at that time and I said, as we were still sitting there, "Bill, I wish to hell I knew who those people are, because it's a good possibility that we are going to miss them."

Bill said quietly, "I know who they are."

"Well, who in the hell are they?"

"The one that left was John Tieder, Jr."

"Oh, is that right? Well, who is the one in the brown hunting clothes?"

"That's Warfield. He's Tieder's head guide."

"Well, who's the one in the green hunting togs?"

"That's my brother!"

Well, the damndest feeling came over me.

"Bill, this is absolutely awful! Well, my God, Bill! I'll tell you what. You stay here and I'll hit 'em. This must be as embarrassing as hell to you!"

"No, Bobby knows better. He's already told me that he killed the limit this morning. In fact, he came to the house and gave me a couple of geese."

"Well, I'll be damned!" I said.

So I went around and drove in there with Bill and Larry covering as much of the field as they could on foot and just about the time I got out of the car (the closest I could get was by this big barn), Ol' Bobby Richardson "caught himself a rabbit." He literally flew across that damned field.

We got Warfield and we got the thirteen geese, but we didn't get Bobby. He just flat ran to the edge of the woods there and disappeared. It was pointless to chase him. We knew who he was. You couldn't get a better witness than a man's brother!

We got the information from Warfield, took the geese back into Cambridge, and I spent the night there.

The next morning, I met Larry and Bill about five o'clock.

"OK, boys, we want to get down there to Tieder's place before dawn. I want to check out this situation. The way those geese were coming in, there has got to be bait out there."

We got at the scene just at the crack of light and we found the bait. It was spread out on the edge of the Choptank River and the geese had to come in over the pit to get to the bait when the wind was blowing northwest at at least twenty-five knots, just as the drunk in that bar had told me!

We found the bait and then we went to John Tieder Jr.'s place.

"Mr. Tieder, I'm Willie Parker, federal game agent. I came to talk to you about that little goose hunt you made yesterday afternoon."

"What about it, Mr. Parker?"

"We were down there this morning and checked the area and it was heavily baited."

"What if I told you I put that bait out last night?"

"Why, hell, you can tell me anything you want to tell me, but it's not going to change the facts. I'm going to take some information from you and I'm going to charge you with shooting over bait in the United States courts."

We wrote John Tieder, Jr., up right there in his very sumptuous home and gave him a summons, then we went on into Cambridge. I left Thurman and Richardson behind.

Bobby Richardson had a half interest in an automobile dealership in the town and I went into his place of business to talk to him.

"Bobby, I want to see you for just a few minutes."

"I've already talked to my lawyer, and I'm not going to tell you a damned thing!"

"Well, I'm not going to ask you any questions other than just your name and address and the number of your hunting license, and all that old jazz. I'm not really going to ask you very much."

"What the hell's the meaning of all this crap?"

"Bobby, you know what the meaning of this is. Yesterday afternoon you killed Canada geese down there on John Tieder, Jr.'s place. It was heavily baited, and I'm going to file charges against you in the United States District Court."

"You'll have hell's own time, Parker, ever proving that I killed any geese on John Tieder, Jr.'s place yesterday!"

"I don't think so, Bobby. It'll be very simple to prove, as a matter of fact."

"Could you identify me? You said a man ran. You said that I ran. How do you know that?"

"Well, I sure can't prove that it was you running across that field, not at that distance, but the man who was with me could."

"Who was with you?"

"Your brother, Bill!"

"My brother, Bill, was with you! Oh, my God! That's bad!"

"Yea, it's bad, Bobby, very bad. It really embarrassed ol' Bill, and it embarrassed me, too. I suggest that you ought to drop down and talk to Bill about this whole damned thing. He really feels badly about it, but I'm still going to file the charges."

I worked the rest of that day in Dorchester County and then went back to Annapolis. I got into the office there pretty late and Bobby Richardson had been trying to get me on the phone for most of that afternoon.

Finally he did get ahold of me and told me, "Mr. Parker, now I want to tell you the whole truth."

"Bobby, don't tell me anything. Just make sure that lawyer you said you talked to is a darn good one."

"I don't want a damned lawyer," he replied. "I want to tell you that I killed those geese or helped to kill them. I didn't know the bait was there, but it sure must have been. I want to make a plea of guilty and just make a clean breast of the whole thing."

Well, after that conversation, or not long after, Bobby Richardson came before the United States magistrate in Baltimore, pleaded guilty, and I think that they fined him four or five hundred dollars and put him on probation for a couple of years, during which time he was not allowed to hunt migratory waterfowl or any species of wildlife protected by the United States.

But this case had a peculiar damn twist, both at the beginning and at the end. While he was on probation, Bobby wrote a hell of a fine book on decoys.

He gave me a copy of the book and I was real pleased with what he inscribed on the flyleaf. "TO MY FRIEND, BILL PARKER. I wrote this book during the two winters I couldn't hunt!"

chapter 20

A
"Hair-Raising" Case

WE HAD WHAT you might call a "hair-raising" case down in southern Maryland during the cold winter of 1970. It was a situation where the canvasback that were using the Wicomico River were getting the living hell shot out of them, and it had to be stopped.

I left Annapolis at three A.M. one bitter morning late in the season. It was spitting snow, and I had to drive about a hundred miles to Leonardtown and meet Maryland Wildlife Officer Bob Arnold. (Leonardtown is the county seat for St. Mary's, Maryland's southernmost county.)

Bob dropped me off on the banks of the river before daylight and I walked about a mile along the shore and positioned myself behind a heavily baited duck blind that had long been under surveillance. I concealed myself in some thick honeysuckle, opened my Thermos, and had a cup of steaming coffee.

After I'd downed several cups of coffee, dawn began to break. No hunters came to the blind. At seven A.M., I started to depart, cursing the dumb luck that appeared to protect some people.

After walking some five hundred yards south of the baited blind, I stopped for a minute to watch the ducks. There were about three hundred canvasbacks feeding furiously about fifty yards in front of the blind I had been watching and in the general area.

Suddenly farther south, from a distance of about three quarters of a mile, I heard fifteen rapid shots. They were so fast they blurred together. Following this barrage, I heard about twenty-five single shots. I heard the singles while I was running, trying to get to the scene as soon as possible.

I knew exactly what had happened. These gunners had emptied

unplugged, auto-loading shotguns into a flock of baited can-vasbacks. Now the single shots that I was hearing were polishing off the cripples.

I hid my portable radio, binoculars, rain gear, and heavy coat in a briar patch and I ran steadily toward the sound of these damn shots. The shooting stopped when I was about halfway there. I was running in hip boots and was tiring as I approached the river point where I thought the shooting had come from. I rounded an old, abandoned farmhouse and saw three men coming up the riverbank.

The first man had his arms full of canvasback ducks. The second was carrying two shotguns, while the third was carrying a shotgun and several boxes of shotgun shells.

They saw me from a distance of about two hundred yards and immediately turned and ran. They split, running in three different directions. I picked out the heaviest of the three and gave chase. He was heading up the river beach and running good. I ran him some six hundred yards and wasn't gaining a foot. To make matters worse, my strength was rapidly waning. It was apparent that I could not overtake him, so I stopped and pulled my three-fifty-seven magnum pistol from its holster and fired into the water some thirty feet to his right. This extremely powerful bullet hit an incoming wave and threw water twenty feet up into the air.

The man stopped immediately and threw up both hands. I quickly closed the remaining distance.

"Turn around!"

I immediately recognized him as a "troubleshooter," Raymond Sylvester Morgan. I knew him as a prominent waterman of the area and had apprehended him on two previous occasions for shooting ducks over bait.

"Please don't shoot me!"

"I'm not going to hurt you. Put your hands down!"

"Agent Parker, you are damned fast on your feet."

"Cut out the crap, Raymond. Who were those two people with you?"

"I don't know who they are!"

"Bullshit! You aren't the type to shoot ducks with perfect strangers!"

"I'll swear that I don't know who they are!"

"OK, Raymond. It suits the hell out of me if you don't want to cooperate. Let's pick up the damn ducks and go."

"Go where?"

"There's a patrol car waiting for me up this river. I intend to put you in that patrol car and haul your ass to the Baltimore city jail. I'll come get you out for arraignment on Monday morning because they don't hold court up there on Saturdays."

"Agent Parker, please don't put me in jail! Do you have to take me in?"

"No, I don't have to take you in, but you don't seem to want to cooperate with me, so why should I show you any consideration?"

The man paused for just a minute. "I'm gonna tell you. It was Robert Pogue and Eugene Latham."

By this time, we had walked to the scene of the shooting. There were still some crippled canvasbacks swimming down the river.

I picked up thirteen dead canvasback from the point where the hunters had run. I picked up five full boxes of twelve-gauge high-velocity shells and some fifty-five freshly fired shells.

"Stay here!" I ordered Morgan, leaving him with the ducks and shells. I followed the tracks of the other two men. About a hundred yards up the beach, I discovered a discarded plaid wool jacket.

I picked this up and continued to follow the tracks. About fifty yards farther along the beach, I found a red cap. I recognized both garments as having been worn by the hunters who had made a break for it.

Finally I lost the tracks and returned to the point where I had left Morgan. When I returned, I also found Bob Arnold at the scene with my patrol car.

We checked the shooting area and were able to determine that it was heavily baited with shelled yellow corn. Morgan admitted baiting the area, stating that he had put out some fifteen hundred pounds of corn in the past two weeks.

Well, Bob and I loaded everything we were seizing into plastic bags, wrote Morgan up, and continued our patrol.

The following Monday, I conferred with my friend, Assistant United States Attorney Michael E. Marr.

"Bill, you'll need more than Morgan's statement to convict the other two. Why don't you take that jacket and hunting hat to the FBI Crime Lab in Washington for examination?"

I did just that the same day, talking with two FBI agents there and making them aware of the importance of the case.

"I need some evidence that will back up the testimony of a codefendant."

They promised complete cooperation.

About a month had passed and I was then informed that they had found three human hairs on the cap and two others on the jacket. They further advised me that if I could obtain hair from the heads of the two suspects, it would be possible to match them and establish identity, but warned me that it may not be positive.

I immediately drove back to Baltimore and conferred with Mike Marr.

"Mike, how in the hell can I get a sample of hair from Latham and Pogue."

"Hell, that's simple. We'll just get a search warrant for their heads."

"That's the damndest thing I ever heard of!" I answered. "But if it's legal, let's get one!"

We went before Chief United States Magistrate Clarence Goetz and obtained arrest warrants for all three of these canvasback killers. We also obtained search warrants for the homes *and heads* of Latham and Pogue!

On the way home that afternoon, I contacted three of my agents by radio.

"Meet me at Leonardtown at eight o'clock tonight and prepare to stay overnight. We have a job to do early in the morning."

"Ten-four, Chief!"

We had the assistance of a deputy United States marshal and we went around to their homes and arrested both Pogue and Latham at dawn the next day. We hauled both of these men to the United States marshal's lockup in Baltimore in handcuffs. Pogue, an officer in a Lexington Park bank, was mad as hell.

In Baltimore the two men were booked and fingerprinted. And under the authority of the search warrant, we searched their heads.

We took a damned generous sample from each head. Both men were admitted to bond and engaged the services of an attorney.

The next morning, I drove to Leonardtown and served an arrest warrant on Morgan. After mugging and fingerprinting, he was released on a personal recognizance bond at my request. Then I drove to Washington and turned over to the FBI the samples of hair, taken under the authority of what was probably one of the strangest search warrants ever issued.

We tried Morgan first simply because we planned to use him for a witness against the others. He entered a plea of guilty and was sentenced to sixty days in jail.

We were waiting for a report from the FBI lab before we scheduled the two other cases. But before we received the report, Assistant United States Attorney Marr was contacted by the attorney who represented Latham and Pogue. He indicated that both of his clients were anxious to come into court and plead guilty. They wanted to get the matter behind them.

Marr agreed to these proceedings. Each of these men was sentenced to a sixty-day jail term and fined five hundred dollars. Robert Pogue and Eugene Latham were also placed on probation for a period of three years. It was "NO HUNTING" for them during this period as far as migratory birds protected by the federal government were concerned.

Some two weeks later, I received a report from the FBI Crime Lab. It stated simply that the results of the test for human hair comparison were inconclusive.

The United States courts were getting tough on violators of the Federal Game Laws. Maryland was no longer a happy hunting ground for the slaughter of waterfowl and dove and other species of game that it was my duty to protect.

We had clearly demonstrated that we could arrest and convict the "big ones." There was no longer the story of the "big one that got away." People in Maryland were now being sent to jail for violating Migratory Bird Laws.

But there was still much to be done. I had been in Maryland for eight years, but it was not in the cards for me to stay and finish the job.

chapter 21

Thrown Back into the Briar Patch

RUMORS WERE CIRCULATING in 1973 that the Department of Interior, Fish and Wildlife Service, was planning to reorganize its law enforcement agencies.

Up to this time, the divisions had been on a regional basis. There were six geographical regions within the United States and each had its own law enforcement division. The regional supervisor was responsible for several states, in fact, probably too many states.

Fred Williams, in the Atlanta Division, was responsible for fourteen southeastern states, as well as Puerto Rico and the Virgin Islands. This is really too much territory for one man to supervise.

The rumors were rife, as is always true in government, about what the reorganization would be. We were finally able to get some information from Washington that the nation was going to be divided into thirteen smaller districts and that a good deal of our direction in the future would come from Washington.

There were several reasons for this move, and the top-level thinking behind it was very good. The smaller divisions would allow more efficient program direction. It would provide a better, closer working relationship between the various districts. They would set up a situation where the thirteen districts could and would cooperate in investigations that crossed state lines.

During these changing times in 1973, the United States Fish and Wildlife Service had selected thirteen cities across the United States for the location of the thirteen central offices. These were to be called Special Agent in Charge offices, SAC.

I looked at one of the first maps they put out on the subject and lo and behold, Baltimore was selected as a regional headquarters! I was intensely interested in staying in the Maryland area. OK, I made a play for that post. But when you filed for one of these new SAC positions, you had to file for all of them!

I stated on my application that I believed I had demonstrated my capability to direct a law enforcement program in Maryland and, since I had valuable contacts on the Atlantic seaboard, it would probably benefit the bureau and certainly myself if they permitted me to remain in the Baltimore area as special agent in charge.

Finally all of the applications that were submitted nationwide were being handled in the Washington office. It was a period when the administrators in the Fish and Wildlife Service of the Department of the Interior were faced with awesome responsibility, because where they placed these men not only greatly affected each man, but his family as well.

They were selecting the thirteen agents in charge and also the thirteen assistant agents. This move would require twenty-six transfers, or close to that. A few people were able to remain in their same positions.

As the time for the reorganization to take effect early in 1974 drew near, I became more and more apprehensive about where they might send me. I began to get some rumors that they, in Washington headquarters, had decided that New York and New Jersey was a major problem area and that headquarters for this new region would be in New York City.

I had about as much desire to go up to New York and New Jersey as I had to take a damned trip to the moon! I had no interest in the Atlantic seaboard north of the state of Maryland or possibly Delaware.

The day of reckoning finally came. I was selected as special agent in charge of the region headquartered in Nashville, Tennessee!

Well, in a sense, this was just like throwing me "back in the briar patch!" I was making a complete circle in my law enforcement work. I had started my career as a state game warden in Tennessee in Robertson County, just north of Nashville, and here I was, home again!

I knew many people in this area and coming back was not at all uncomfortable. I was to be responsible for the states of Tennessee,

Kentucky (where I had done much work earlier in my career), and North and South Carolina.

Because I knew Tennessee and Kentucky so well, I didn't, in 1974, envision any difficulty in establishing a rather effective game law enforcement program in those two states.

However, I had never worked in either North or South Carolina. I knew little or nothing about these states except where they were located. It would take some real effort to establish the type of program I wanted here.

Well, I came to Nashville on the twenty-sixth day of May 1974 and assumed responsibility for this four-state district. We had a little old office out on West End Avenue, which was smaller than my present kitchen in my new home in Donelson, a suburb of Nashville. There was no clerical help, no administrative help, nothing but myself and a four-state district!

I didn't have but nine agents working in the entire district, and four of them retired almost immediately after the new setup went into effect. That left me with only five federal game wardens in a four-state field.

Well, the summer of 1974 went by quickly, June, July, and August, in rapid succession. During that period, I made arrangements with the General Services Administration for a modern office on the ninth floor of the Federal Building annex on Broad Street in Nashville.

We hired some very competent clerical assistants, an administrative assistant, and laid the groundwork for an effective law enforcement program, dealing basically with the mechanics and organization of a modern-day law enforcement operation.

chapter **22**

The Hiring of
A Lady Agent

In 1975, I became interested in the possibilities of using female law enforcement agents. We have always wanted to place those from the so-called minority groups into responsible positions.

So, I began to recruit for a female agent. I must have interviewed possibly fifty or sixty people. Some I interviewed in person and some by telephone.

And the more I interviewed, the more I felt that there was no way that I could possibly find a woman who would be able to handle the full responsibility of a special agent of the United States Fish and Wildlife Service. My interviews were rather brutal because any woman who applied had to hear precisely what she was going to be faced with and what I would expect from her and what she would have to do to be successful as a special agent of the Fish and Wildlife Service.

In May of 1975, I received a telephone call from a girl in Washington, D.C. She told me her name was Lucinda Delaney. "Lucinda" . . . a most unlikely name for a special agent! She wanted to come to Nashville at her own expense for an interview. She told me that she had a degree in police administration from the University of Maryland and that she was working in the Washington, D.C., office of the U.S. Fish and Wildlife Service but she was relegated to the "Hey, You!" activities: "Hey, You! Go get me this," "Hey, You, get me that!" "Go file this for me" and all that kind of jazz and she wasn't satisfied with that. She wanted to move into a field position where she could exercise full responsibilities as a special agent with the United States Fish and Wildlife Service.

Well, with a great deal of doubt, I told her to come on to Nashville and that I would be glad to talk with her.

I met her at the Nashville airport one morning about nine

o'clock, and she immediately picked me out. When I saw her, I had this old feeling again: There was absolutely no way a woman could fill the field responsibilities of a fish and wildlife agent. She was about five feet two, weighed about 115 pounds, was blond and very attractive. These just weren't the qualities that I was looking for at that time in a special agent.

I drove her to our office in the Federal Building on Broad Street in Nashville, Tennessee, and subjected her to about a four-and-a-half-hour interview. This interview was extremely brutal because I wanted to discourage her, have her withdraw her application as a special agent in my district.

As the interview progressed, the way she began to answer some questions amazed me. I began to think, "Well, maybe my original impression might have been wrong and that this *was* the 'lady agent' whom I had been looking for."

One of the questions that I put to her was tongue in cheek, and her response was unbelievable.

"Miss Delaney, you say you can handle the responsibilities as a special agent?"

"Yes, sir, I can!"

"Well, what are you going to do if you encounter a two-hundred-and-fifty-pound obnoxious drunk in a duck blind and it becomes absolutely necessary that you take him into custody. *What* are you going to do?"

Her response was, "I don't know, Mr. Parker. But I'll do something!"

Well this intrigued me because she was small and not physically able to handle a big, tough hunter, but then I looked at her and figured that with *her* determination, she *would* do something!

As the interview progressed, I saw that her intelligence, her common sense, combined with her formal education, made her appear to be just exactly the kind of person that I was looking for; but I wanted to be sure. I told her how cold the weather could be, how wet she'd get, and that she'd be working with male agents exclusively, both state and federal.

"Miss Delaney, I don't plan on walking back five miles to where I started from to take a leak if I have to relieve myself. I'd just turn my back. You won't be getting any special privileges in the field."

I wanted her to know precisely what she would be faced with. "We work long hard hours in cold, wet, remote marshes and the calls of nature come to us just as they do for other people."

"This will cause me no problem, Mr. Parker." That little good-looking blond sitting across the desk from me didn't blink an eye!

I also told her, "Because you are young and very attractive, every son of a bitch you associate with will make a pass at you. Can you handle this?" I asked her.

"Yes, I can handle anything!"

Well, the interview in the office terminated about three o'clock. We went to the patrol car and I took her to my house on the way back to the airport to give her an opportunity to meet my wife and family.

My wife, Faye, has been exposed to special agent work for more than twenty years and if there ever was an authority on the subject, she certainly is.

I wanted Mrs. Parker to talk to Lucinda; she could tell her of some of the delicate aspects of this work as far as a girl is concerned that I wasn't able to tell her. My wife whipped it on her and whipped it on her good.

About four-thirty, I drove Miss Delaney back to the airport. When we got there about twenty minutes before her plane left, she said, "Well, Mr. Parker, I do appreciate your time, but I feel that I have miserably failed my interview."

"Quite the contrary, Miss Delaney. Quite the contrary. You are the first woman I have interviewed for the job who has interested me. I am impressed by your attitude. If you apply for the position, I intend to select you for it."

I still had a hell of a feeling of trepidation about putting a 115-pound girl out in the rough district that I represent. I knew well that she was going to be faced with some bad situations that would "set the hair" on even the bravest male. I had no way of knowing what her response to these things was going to be.

I finally got Miss Delaney assigned as a special agent to my district in August of 1975. I stationed her at Raleigh, North Carolina.

She came rolling into Raleigh in a Toyota with all her possessions in a little trailer hooked behind. She rented her an apartment and reported in, ready to go to work.

She had to be taught everything. She became quite proficient with the use of a pistol.

We use some big outboard engines and some very fast boats in our work and they are dangerous in the hands of an inexperienced operator. Through our personnel in North Carolina, we immediately began a training process for Miss Delaney. We taught her how to handle fast outboards. We made her comfortable in float planes and helicopters. We were quite satisfied with her ability to handle fast powerful patrol cars. Her response to training was very good, but we had a hell of a problem finding hip boots and waders that would fit her! She had a size four or five foot and they don't normally make waders that small! We finally located sufficient rubber gear for her that fit, through a mail-order house.

When the dove season opened in North Carolina, I conferred with our personnel over there and they asked, "What do you want us to do, keep an agent with her all the time?"

I said, "No, turn her loose, kick her out of the nest. I will monitor her activities and see how she reacts to these situations."

Well, she was the damndest thing that ever hit the hunting scene in North Carolina. On the opening day of the dove season over there, she hit a baited dove field. And she put a bunch of prominent North Carolina businessmen and hunters into a state of shock when she walked into that field and announced that her name was Delaney and she was a special agent with the United States Fish and Wildlife Service, and that field was baited and they were in a peck of damn trouble. Well, they grouped around her . . . they looked at her . . . they examined her credentials . . . they walked around . . . they were absolutely astounded. She handled the matter exceptionally well!

She took the information, told the people they would be advised where and when to appear in court, and bid them good-day.

She collected evidence, she photographed the area, she handled the situation in an unusually professional fashion.

Violators that Miss Delaney caught went into a state of shock! Usually they thought she was a boy, because she wore men's clothing in the field. But, hell, it was quite easy for them to determine, even on a cursory inspection, that she wasn't a boy! This further compounded their feelings.

On one difficult waterfowl assignment in North Carolina, I was working with my "Lady Agent."

I woke Agent Delaney up at her motel room at three A.M. on a bitter winter morning. The wind was blowing strong, it was about fifteen degrees above zero and she came out looking very sleepy but ready to go in her "work" clothes.

"What do you have under those pants?" I asked her.

"Nothing but the usual, Mr. Parker."

"Didn't I tell you to get some insulated underwear?"

"Yes, sir."

"Well, where are they?"

"In there," she motioned to her motel room.

"Agent Delaney, go back in there and put them on and hurry! We have to get going." Her motel room was in Newport, N.C.

She returned a few moments later and we put the open boat overboard, preparing for a long, wet, and very cold trip before daylight, on the Neuse River, a few miles north of her motel.

I could tell that Agent Delaney was shivering. I could hear her teeth chattering before we had been gone very long.

I spoke loudly and perhaps my voice sounded harsh against the wind.

"Are you cold, Agent Delaney?"

"NO, SIR! Mr. Parker, I'm not cold!"

We continued our mission; it took the entire day, and the next morning I got her out again at three A.M.

She never made one sound of protest. Not a complaint about being either tired or cold, yet I knew damn well that she was both!

Well, she made the inevitable mistakes that young agents make ... you can expect it. She fell out of the damn boat when it was about eighteen or nineteen degrees and got soaking wet. She was instructed to empty her hip boots, wring out her outer clothing, and put them back on and go back to work . . . and she did just that. She fell out of the boat about seven o'clock in the morning and she worked until seven o'clock that night, in wet clothes.

I had told her when we had selected her for the position in North Carolina that there were two things that would get her in serious trouble: If she ever told me that she was cold or if she ever told me that she was tired . . . I would fire her . . . immediately!

The news of Cindy's success crossed the nation as news invariably does (we have a hell of a grapevine in Fish and Wildlife circles). Most of the law enforcement districts in the damn country wanted her reassigned. She will work throughout the United States within the next few years as a result of this.

We have utilized her in many covert operations . . . some are continuing at this time that I can't discuss.

chapter 23

How to "Skin" Alligator Skinners

DAVID HALL, MY assistant in Nashville during 1974, but now special
agent in charge in New Orleans, is a professional undercover agent
whose equal I have yet to see. Dave had been prowling around over
North Carolina and he had come up with some information that
there was a ring of alligator poachers operating in North Carolina
and South Carolina. Well, we knew that North Carolina had a
fringe population of the American alligator and that South
Carolina is loaded with the American alligators.

Dave went to work on this case. He established contact with these
poachers over there through an undercover agent who had no idea
who Dave was or what he was doing. Dave set them up good. He
made arrangements to meet them at a motel in Smithfield, North
Carolina, one afternoon. He was posing as a major alligator dealer.

Dave had gone to Louisiana and set up a foolproof background
because we knew that these people were organized to the extent that
they would check him out. We just couldn't give a bogus telephone
and address.

As it turned out, they checked him so closely that one of their
representatives went to Louisiana and checked the physical site
where this alligator-tanning operation was supposed to be going on.
Fortunately we had set Dave's cover-up at an alligator tannery. It
worked.

The original contact with three subjects—Pruitt, Jackson, and
Small—was in a motel at Smithfield, North Carolina. Dave, of
course, couldn't go armed. A gun would be a giveaway; it would be
noticed. We knew by local reputation that these people were tough.

At this motel meeting, I wanted Dave to have considerable
protection, so I had Special Agent Perry White accompany him.

I decided that Dave still needed additional coverage. I made arrangements to borrow a fine girl out of the United States attorney's office at Raleigh, North Carolina.

I wanted this girl to go with me to Smithfield where Dave was supposed to meet the men who were dealing in illegal alligator skins. We would have dinner at an adjoining table where I could keep an eye on things and give Dave the protection he might damn well need.

It was quite humorous, in a sense, because I didn't tell this girl just what she would be involved in.

When she saw me strap a thirty-eight special under my left arm, underneath a sports coat, she asked, "What's that for?"

"That's just insurance!"

"What for?"

"We've got a situation where we are making an undercover contact with some people who are dealing in illicit alligator skins and I want you for a cover. I want us to appear to be having dinner at this restaurant. You just don't say anything unless I ask you a question."

She agreed to do that. She was quite thrilled and I guess it *was* unusual for her to be in this position.

We went in this restaurant and took our position at a table in the middle of a huge dining room. They served a buffet dinner. We went through the buffet line, then sat at our table and ate.

We were almost finished eating and were working on our dessert and coffee when Dave Hall came in with these three characters. Well, Dave and these three sat down at a table adjacent to us. We were close enough to hear them talk, to overhear most of their conversation. They were wheeling and dealing raw alligator skins, trying to agree on a price.

Suddenly a surprising thing happened! There was a young couple over in the corner who were real dressed up. As it turned out, they had just got married and had stopped there for dinner. One of them snapped a picture of the other, using a flashbulb. The minute that happened, two of the men who were sitting with Dave sprang from their table and went straight over to this couple.

"What did you take a picture of?"

"Why I . . . I . . . just took a picture of my new wife!"

"What direction was that camera pointing? Was it pointing toward our table?"

"No, sir!"

"Well, all right then."

They went back and sat down.

This caused me a little bit of concern. If a man doesn't want his picture taken, he's got a good reason for that and the way they came up from that table made it appear that they were ready for just about anything!

After we finished our dinner, we sat there and drank coffee until Dave and these people finished their coffee, and possibly pie. They didn't have dinner.

Then they left the restaurant and went to Dave's motel room.

As they were beginning to leave, we hurried out. This young lady and I went to my motel room across the court where I could watch the men with Dave through binoculars.

We drew the drapes and left a small opening that I could watch through to see what in the hell was going on across that motel court.

This fellow pulled up in a new Lincoln Continental, a Mark IV. He opened the trunk and took out a big ice chest and he took that chest into Hall's room. We moved carefully outside. This was simply to furnish better cover. I was heavily armed with a three-fifty-seven magnum. I knew that Dave wasn't, nor was Perry White. In case anything erupted, I was to bail them out in a hurry.

Fortunately the cover wasn't blown. Dave bought about $195 worth of raw alligator skins. He said he wanted to study the quality of the skins before he placed a big order.

He paid the people for the skins, and they departed.

We waited for some thirty or forty minutes. Then I drove this young lady back to Raleigh and dropped her off.

I returned to the motel, and we inspected the merchandise. Dave had bought some prime alligator skins, some five- and six-foot long. He was paying about eleven dollars a linear foot for them.

We left Smithfield and went on back to Nashville, and Dave set this group up for a large delivery. He wanted the skins delivered to

New Orleans, Louisiana, to his tannery. These people agreed to deliver to Dave seven or eight hundred alligator skins to a certain place at a certain date and time.

Dave was waiting for them when they arrived. They came in a new tractor and trailer. They backed into this place and they started unloading alligator skins. Dave had a couple of fellows to help him. They were grading the skins and counting them and the total take on this deal was to be about eighteen hundred dollars. We don't have that kind of money, so we had to move in before the deal was consummated.

Our agents hit the group. They arrested the two men from North Carolina who hauled the alligator skins down there. They also took Dave Hall into custody. They handcuffed Dave Hall. They handcuffed the two subjects. They handcuffed the other fellows who were trying to help Dave count and grade those skins.

They hauled them all immediately to a New Orleans jail and locked them up—they locked Dave Hall in the same cell with the black marketeers.

Well, these men were astounded that anything like this could have occurred. Something had happened. Someone, somewhere had got wind of this and had tipped the Feds off. They had been hit!

Dave spent one night and one day in the bullpen with these two North Carolina alligator poachers. They, thinking that he was also in custody, and in as much trouble as they were, talked freely to Dave. He got the whole picture.

The agents seized the truck and trailer under the authority of the Endangered Species Act, and those rigs cost a hell of a lot of money. They also seized the load of alligator skins.

Some few days later these men made bond. They hired themselves some very good attorneys and they went back to North Carolina.

Six months later they, through their attorney, petitioned the United States District Court of Louisiana for a Rule Twenty procedure, meaning that they can plead in their home jurisdiction.

David Hall went there to North Carolina as the sole witness for the United States government and took the stand because we had to substantiate our allegations before the court would accept the plea.

After Dave's testimony was finished, the United States district judge fined the two principals five thousand dollars each and gave them a long period of highly specialized probation. He fined the man who owned the truck a thousand dollars and gave him a period of specialized probation.

Those two poachers, sitting there in the courtroom while Dave Hall testified, looked mighty unhappy. This one case eliminated the illegal alligator traffic between North and South Carolina.

chapter 24

The Killing of an Eagle

SINCE I HAVE made "the complete circle" and have returned to the place, if not the position, from which I started back in 1949, I have felt, as much as seen, the subtle changes in the public attitude as far as our natural resources are concerned. Although there have always been dedicated people who have cared about our wildlife, their ranks are growing and their voices are being heard. The courts, too, are showing extreme distaste for destructive practices and are developing a philosophy for protection of those endangered species.

A bald eagle was killed at Reelfoot Lake in Tennessee in January of 1975. We had a description of the person who killed that eagle, and we recovered the bird.

The press in west and middle Tennessee kept the story alive for several weeks, and we launched an investigation that was probably the most comprehensive that has ever been launched in the enforcement of wildlife law.

We interviewed nearly 750 people in thirteen west-Tennessee counties. We had narrowed the search for the individual to Shelby County and our list of suspects to five individuals.

We were interviewing these five individuals when one of the five (he was a very prominent surgeon) walked into the United States attorney's office in Memphis.

"I'm the one who killed that eagle." He gave the United States attorney a full statement after being advised of his constitutional rights.

"My children were with me when I killed that eagle, and now my situation at home and with my neighbors has become intolerable as a result of this unfortunate incident."

He had come forward to make all of this known because he wanted to get the matter closed once and for all.

He was immediately scheduled for trial before Chief Judge Bailey Brown for the Western District of Tennessee just one week from the day he had come in to make his admission.

He entered a plea of guilty and was fined one thousand dollars for killing a southern bald eagle.

Now the fine is not significant, nor is even the fact that one eagle was killed. That was an incident in the constant battle that is being waged to protect the endangered species of wildlife in this country.

That incident was closed, or should have been, with the administration of justice in the United States District Courts. But the significant thing about this case is that it didn't stop in the courts.

This man was harassed unmercifully by the public. He was harassed to the extent that the Memphis police had to keep this surgeon's home under armed guard twenty-four hours a day and had to keep his office under guard as well, because the public was so incensed that he had killed an eagle.

chapter 25

The Road Ahead

Two GROUPS OF people in the United States have been highly important to the protection and wise use of our renewable wildlife resources. One is the conservation officer. The other is the American hunter and especially the American waterfowl hunter, who is due one hell of a lot of credit in protecting the species.

Throughout my career as a wildlife officer for some 30 years, in both state and federal law enforcement work, the interested, conservation-minded waterfowl hunter stands beside me and all the people who carry our badges.

Over the years, many of these sportsmen have placed themselves in great personal jeopardy in efforts to end destructive practices for all time.

The majority of people who hunt waterfowl throughout the United States are dedicated sportsmen and women, and conservationists.

They take only a few waterfowl, they abide by the law, and they are concerned about the future. They are the people who are basically responsible for the flocks of migratory waterfowl coming from the North and transversing this country annually.

Without them and the wildlife officer, there would be no hope for future flights of waterfowl, no hope for other species of wildlife, no hope for this part of our American heritage.

But there is a serious problem within the ranks of the protectors of our wildlife.

In 1966, we had a staff of about 170 special federal fish and wildlife agents in the United States, and we were basically responsible for the enforcement of the Migratory Bird Treaty Act. Of course, we were also responsible for enforcing a few other federal laws.

In the years since then, the responsibilities of the federal fish and wildlife agents have increased tenfold by amendments to the Migratory Bird Treaty Act to include some thirty-two species of birds now on the federally protected list as a result of an agreement with Mexico and other countries. For the first time, hawks and owls have come under federal protection.

In 1973, the Endangered Species Act was passed, giving this division of the Department of the Interior, the Fish and Wildlife Service, an awesome task.

The Black Bass Act has been amended. Now almost every creature on this earth is protected by some sort of law that we in the federal agency are responsible for enforcing.

During these same years, our staff has been reduced some twenty percent through attrition and not filling vacant posts. We actually have fewer federal fish and wildlife agents on duty now than we had back in 1966.

I am constantly amazed at the performance of the agents who work for the United States Fish and Wildlife Service. I am heartened by their dedication, ingenuity, and just plain guts. They will push themselves to the limit of physical exhaustion to protect the wildlife resources of this nation.

When I see the young agents who are coming into the law enforcement division of fish and wildlife (although there are not enough of them), how enthusiastic and well motivated they are, then I am heartened and feel that the future of our wildlife resources of the United States of America is in good hands.

I see amazing changes taking place within the law enforcement division of the United States Fish and Wildlife Service. There will be new procedures, new techniques of law enforcement that will be so sophisticated that the "troubleshooter" won't have much of a chance. There will be broader use of electronics, of aircraft, and of treaties with other countries that will enable the federal wildlife law enforcement agent to go *beyond* boundaries of geography just as he now goes beyond the boundaries of human endurance in his commitment.

The Worldwide War for Wildlife shall be won, and that's the last damned word I'm going to say on the subject.